The making of Mike Oldfield's

TUBULAR BELLS

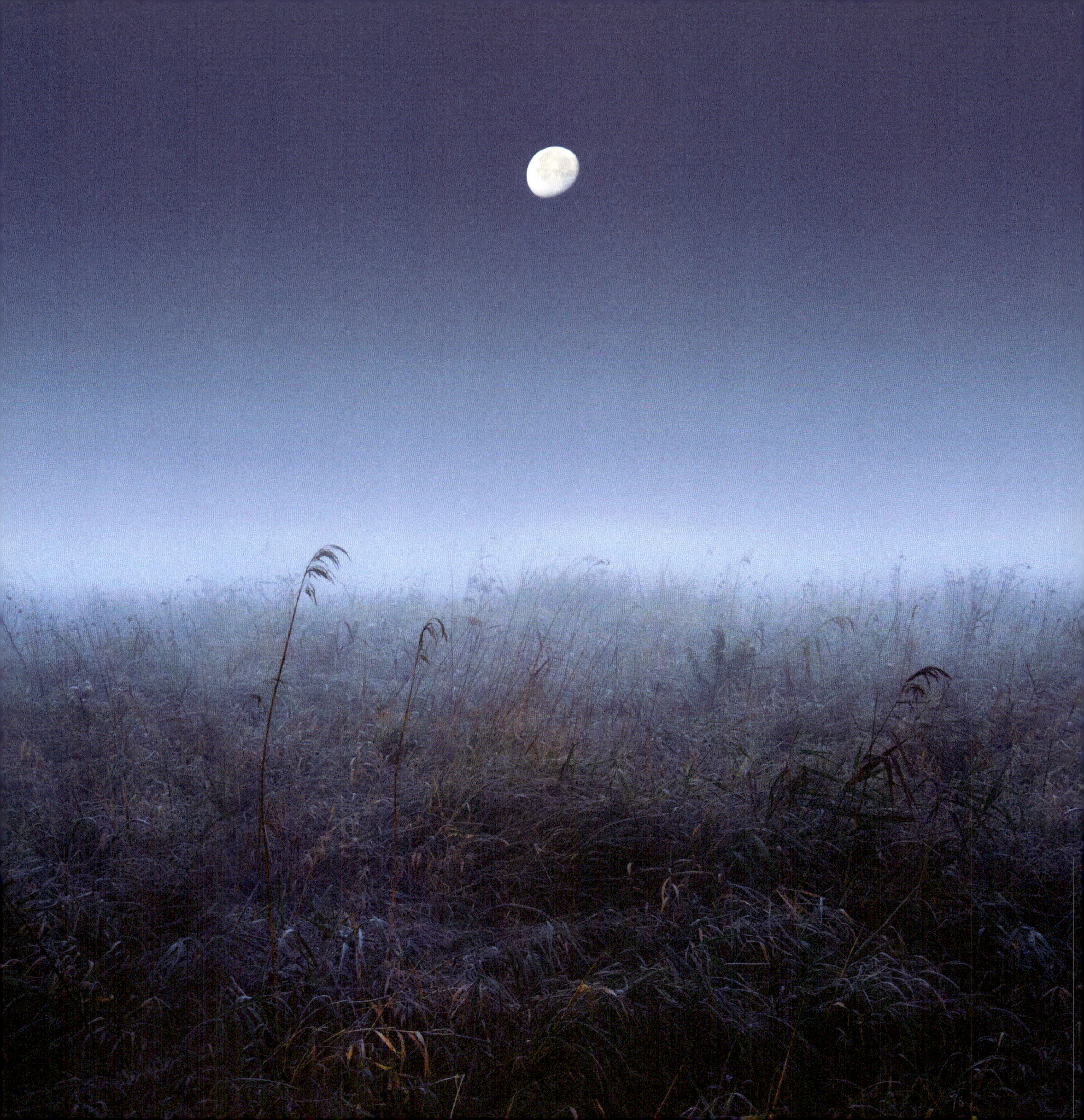

The making of Mike Oldfield's

TUBULAR BELLS

The true story of making the classic 1973 album, as told on the 20th anniversary of its original release

By Richard Newman

Photography by Fran May and Simon Heyworth

storm

storm

The book is published by Storm Music and Images Ltd
Forsters House
Church Hill
Freshford
BA27TX

ISBN: 978-1-9998338-0-0

Produced by Brown Dog Books, Bath, UK
Design by Design Deluxe, Bath, UK
Printed and bound in the UK

This book is dedicated to Fran May and Hannah Kvan.

A special thank-you to Dave Laing for his help with this project.

ABOUT FRAN MAY

FRAN STUDIED photography at the Royal College of Art in the 1970s. The famous documentarian, Bill Brandt was her personal tutor. She received the Vogue Prize for her social documentary images of the East End of London. This led to an international career in documentary, editorial, corporate and fine art photography.

Richard and Fran met when they combined their skills to create an arts rock music project. The result is a book titled 'Brave On Lady' with music CDs at the back of the book.

The music features Richard's extraordinary, impassioned, lead electric guitar playing. Fran's early social documentary photography 1974-78 illustrates the story. The songs document the decade 2007 to 2017. Both periods of time experienced economic uncertainty.

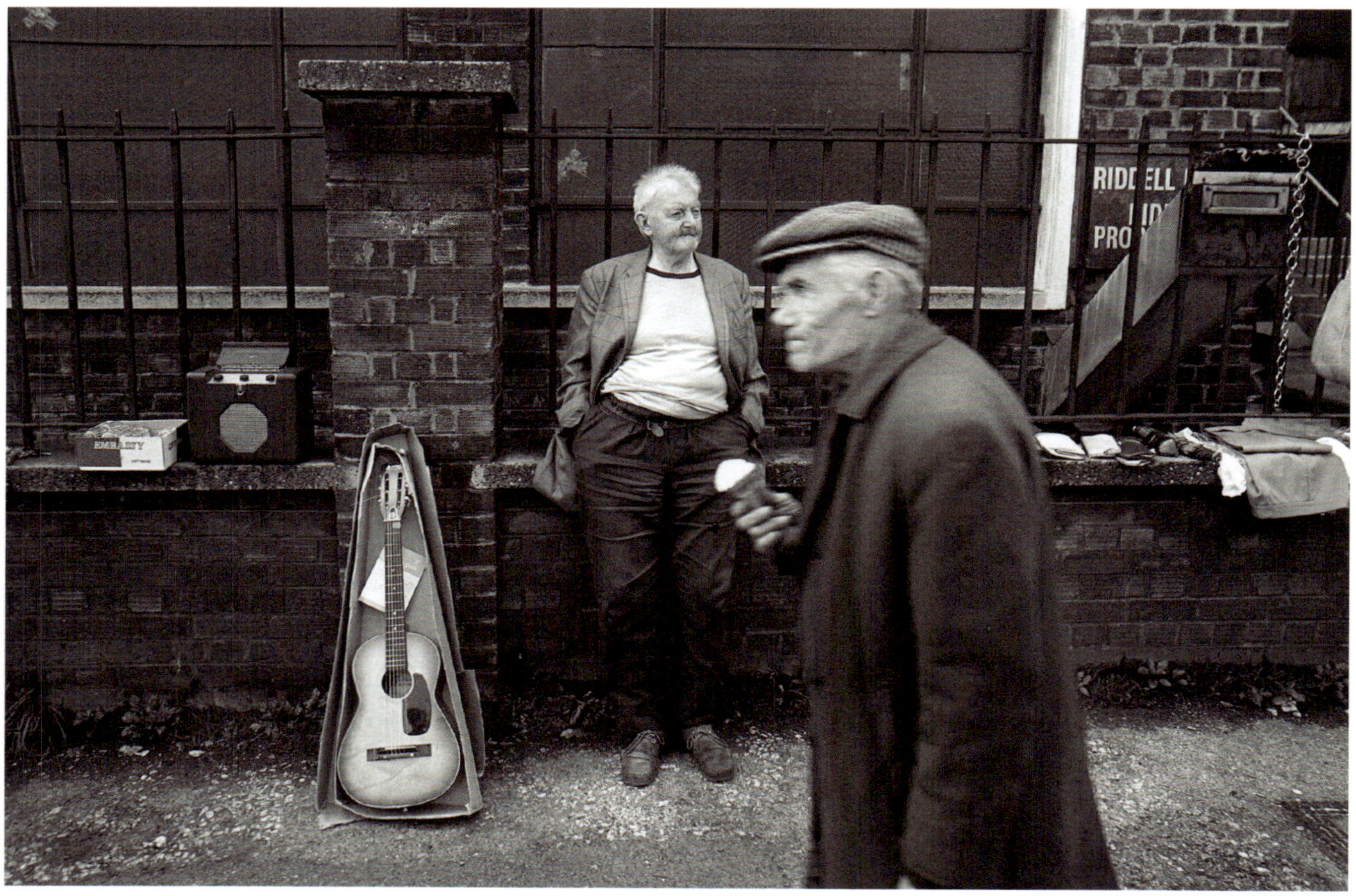

PHOTO: FRAN MAY

One of the images that inspired the song 'Brick Lane'

ABOUT RICHARD NEWMAN

I FIRST MET Richard Newman in the mid-1970s when I was a folk music correspondent for the late-lamented Sounds magazine. At that time, his big idea was the £500 album and he was bursting with ideas to get more music recorded and more music to the people. Richard had already begun to make a name for himself as an interviewer through an all-night programme called 'Night Flight' in the early days of Capital Radio.

In subsequent years he has been one of the great animators of English acoustic and electric music, tireless in his work as a film-maker, record producer, guitar teacher and writer. He even found time to make a couple of very good albums of his own music.

This book is proof that Richard Newman has not lost his genius as an interviewer. He has the rare talent and ability to get musicians to open up and talk about their work, perhaps because he is a gifted musician himself.

He has used that talent brilliantly in this book, which is the best kind of tribute to one of the great landmarks of English music.

DAVE LAING
Co-author, 'The Faber Companion to 20th-Century Popular Music'

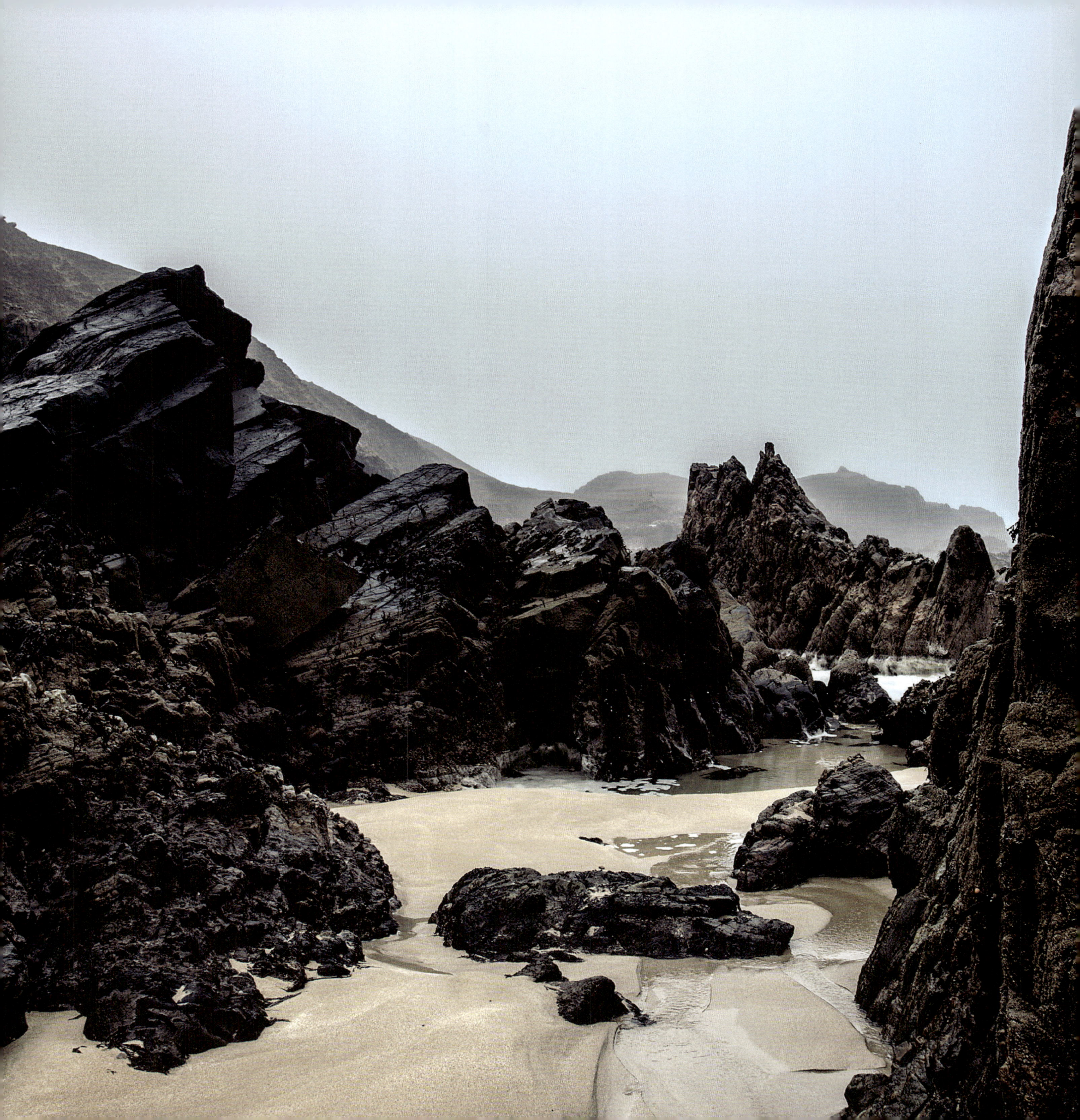

CONTENTS

INTRODUCTION

This is Richard Newman here, and I would like to welcome you to this book.

In 1993 I conducted a series of interviews with the three principal people that created 'Tubular Bells'.

Simon Heyworth, Tom Newman and Mike Oldfield had never met with an independent writer to talk about the creation of the album.

First, I interviewed Tom Newman and Mike Oldfield together. Then I executed an in-depth interview with Tom Newman alone. Last, an interview with Simon Heyworth and Tom Newman together. 1993 was the 20th anniversary year of the publishing of the original 'Tubular Bells' album.

An in-depth approach resulted in many hours of taped interviews. It became an investigation into both the creation of the art and the synchronicity, which led to the formation of Virgin Records.

It is now 2017 and 44 years since the release of the original 'Tubular Bells' album. I've always been a great fan of the original record and I was 23 years old when I bought my copy in 1973.

In 2018 I will have spent five decades in the music industry. I have been a producer, guitarist, songwriter, author, broadcaster and journalist. To celebrate my five decades I decided I wanted to do something special. I wanted to publish these interviews so that everybody, and there are 20 million people who have bought a copy of 'Tubular Bells', could read about the creation of the work, straight from the mouths of the people who made it.

In 2007 I met Fran May, a photographer who had studied at the Royal College of Art. While she was there she won the Vogue Prize for her documentary work.

Years ago, I had written two guitar instruction methods, which I've never published. I needed some students who could be lab rats for me to try out my guitar teaching methods, to see if they still worked.

One of the first people to turn up at my door, having seen the ad, was Fran May. Fran arrived with a red Stratocaster, which had belonged to her late husband. I played Fran some DVDs of guitarists with a view to discovering what kind of music she would like to play. She sat there and watched these DVDs, one of which featured Bonnie Raitt, the American guitarist, who played a Stratocaster. I asked Fran with enthusiasm, "Would you like to play guitar like that?" Her reply was: "No, I would like to do that!"

As she talked to me, it became obvious that she had a plan in her head for a major project. It would link photography with 'Rock Music'. This project became known as 'Brave On Lady'. She described it as being a kind of 'Dark Side of the Moon'. In this case it would be about the lives of women, as seen from Fran's perspective.

Fran asked me if I would be able to help her do this project as a musician, songwriter and producer. As I started to work with her, I began to see some of her amazing photography. Right from the start there were two aspects of this photography that had a deep effect on me. In the first instance, her images of Brick Lane in London and the other was her stunning landscape photography.

These landscape images have a mythological aspect to them. They reveal elemental forces of light, wind, colour, water and the beauty of the English landscape.

Over the years of creating with her on the major cross-arts project, 'Brave On Lady' these images were never far away.

When I started to think about the idea of releasing the interviews about the making of 'Tubular Bells', something occurred to me.

From my point of view the opening 10 minutes of 'Tubular Bells' is an invitation into a world of mythology, magic and deep emotions. Somehow it could be felt and I know for a fact that many, many people have remained affected by this music over the years in that way.

I asked Fran if she would contribute some of her images to this book. I wanted a visual representation of the deep emotions and energy that I felt were present in the music.

The making of 'Tubular Bells' has in itself become a part of studio legend. Back in those days, in 1973, there was no such thing as studio automation. It was all manual work. The story of how they achieved the outcome is well told in the book, but it still amazes me whenever I read it again. It also means so much to so many fans.

This is the story of coincidence. It is also the story of the commitment of three different men, who worked against all the odds to realise the music that lived in Mike Oldfield's head.

Mike had suffered rejection by everybody. All the people in the record companies thought they knew better and tried their hardest to put Mike straight. It needed vocals, it needed drums, it was not commercial, nobody would buy it etc etc.

Well, they were all wrong: lots and lots of us went out to our local record shop and got a copy.

Enjoy the story and the images, but most of all thank you, Mike, Simon and Tom, for the music.

RICHARD NEWMAN
Cambridgeshire 2017

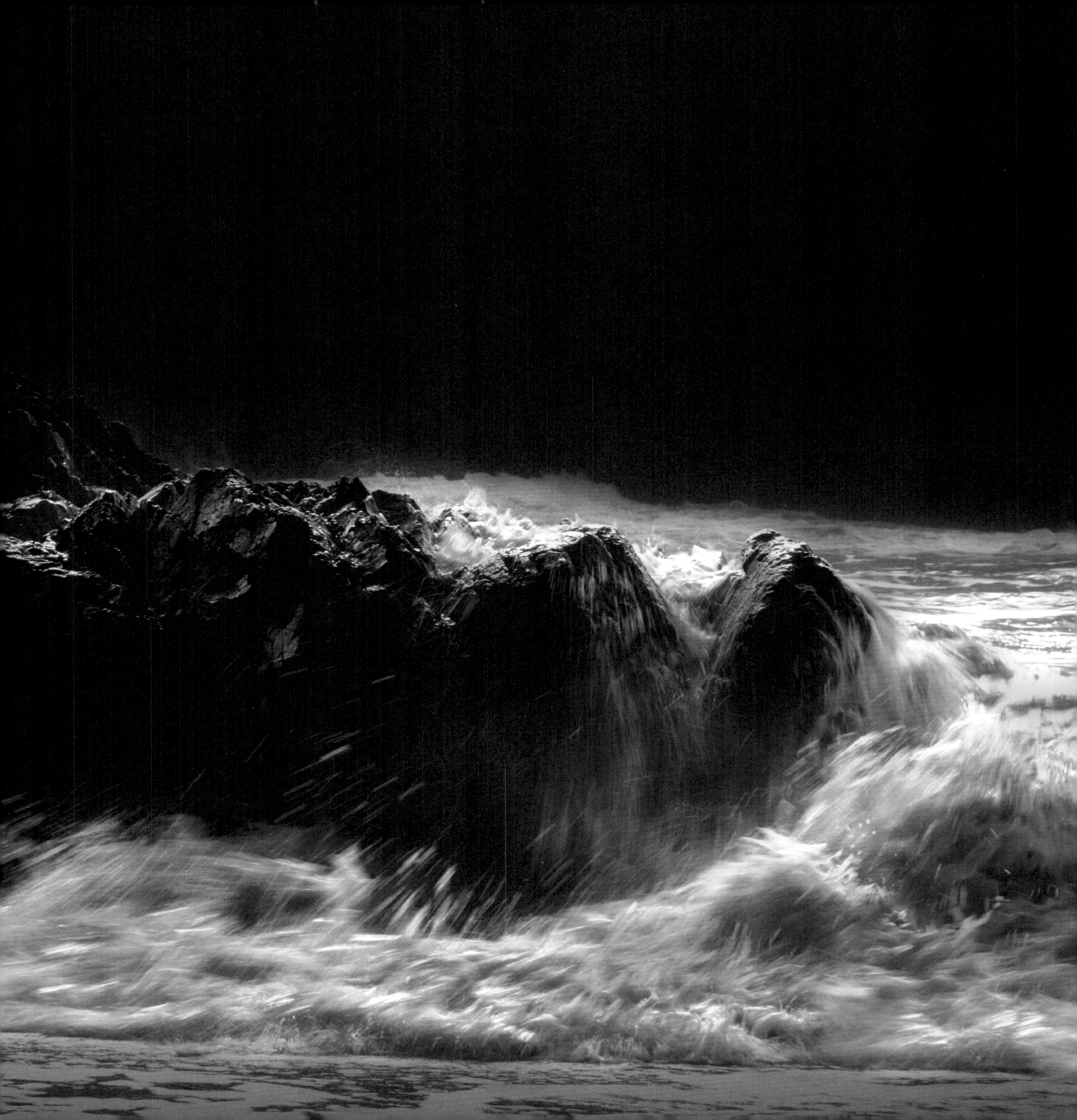

“

There is something about the mythological side to the music that has always interested me. I think there is something in it that is much more enduring than people think. It has the sense of something very old and something very ancient.

It's also very specific to the time in a cultural aspect as well. To contrast it you had the space age mythology of Pink Floyd and I think that 'Tubular Bells' balances that out very well in terms of where it fits into the progress of music.

That is what interests me and I began to look into this when I spoke to his brother (Terry Oldfield) because I realised his brother was actually the great knowledge. Mike was trying to convey this; Mike was the vehicle for it, but I think that the intellectual side of it came from his brother. He told me a lot of things about Celtic mythology and a lot of things that he believed were inherent in the music and so I was sort of right but I always felt that. It was like when I heard the first tune, when I walked down the stairs on that morning, which I will never forget, and heard the opening tune coming out of the room and walking in and seeing Mike sitting on the floor with the old Beocord (reel-to-reel stereo tape deck of the time). It's like it struck a very ancient chord in me and I think that's what it does to people. I'm sure of it.

It is a very beautiful piece, it takes you through many different types of emotions and I think that that is its enduring quality. SIMON HEYWORTH

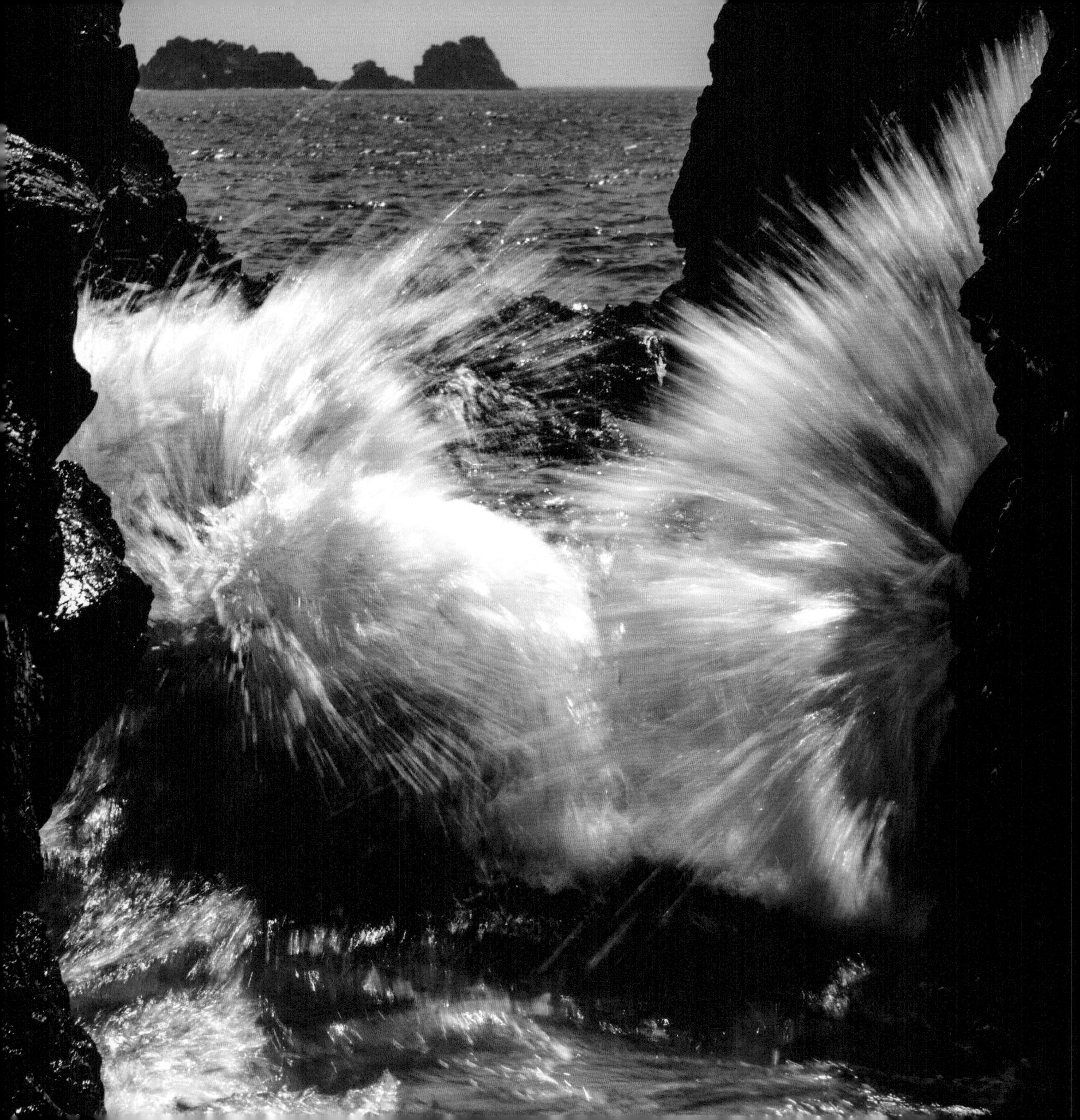

1

THE PROLOGUE

An insight into the music industry at the time of the recording of 'Tubular Bells' in 1973 by Richard Newman

TO SET THE SCENE on the background which made 'Tubular Bells' possible we have to step back to the England of the late '50s and early '60s, when pop music was little more than an indulgence of youth; an expected part of growing up which no one took particularly seriously.

Youth clubs had begun to sprout up all over the country and a skiffle boom introduced artists such as Tommy Steele and Lonnie Donegan to an enthusiastic generation of young people. The media gave a certain amount of space to the phenomenon of pop music, but coverage tended to be patronising; this was not serious art, it was something to be tolerated but never encouraged. The hope was that young people would rapidly grow out of this phase and then settle down to the serious business of education.

Looking at the musical and lyrical content of early pop, it's not surprising that the media sophisticates heaped their scorn. The songs were largely trivial: simple chord structures and subject matter such as boy meets girl, girl leaves boy, boy finds another girl, happy ending etc.

Also in post-war Britain, a whole generation of young males still had conscription to look forward to. This meant that a crucial part of their late-teens and early 20s would be given over to serving in the armed forces. By the beginning of the '60s, however, conscription had been abolished. Arguably this single fact had as much to do with the growth of popular music in the UK as any other.

PHOTO: SIMON HEYWORTH

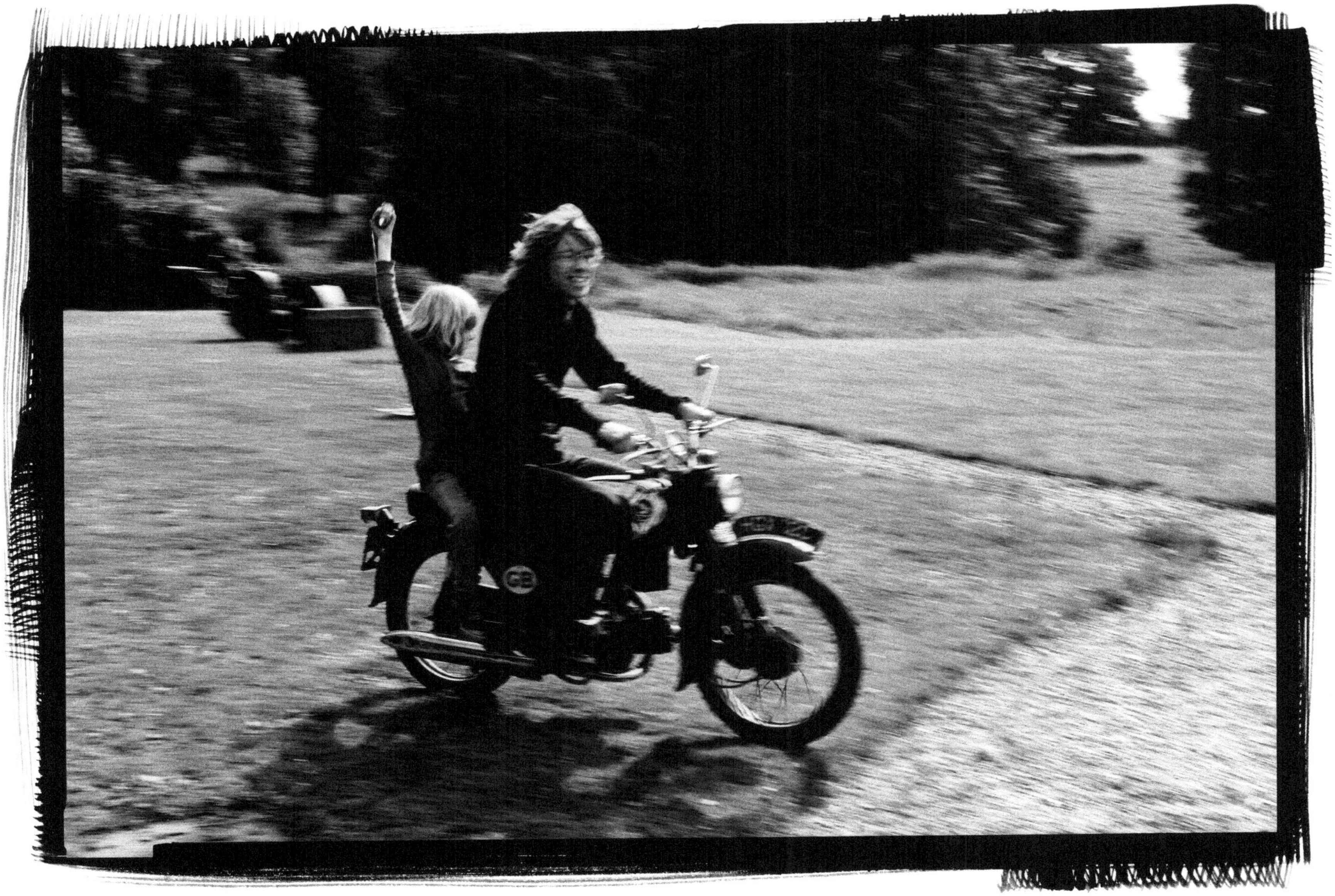

Tom Newman: "Richard Branson … would come down and be the gay young squire … he would entertain the bands by acting the fool"

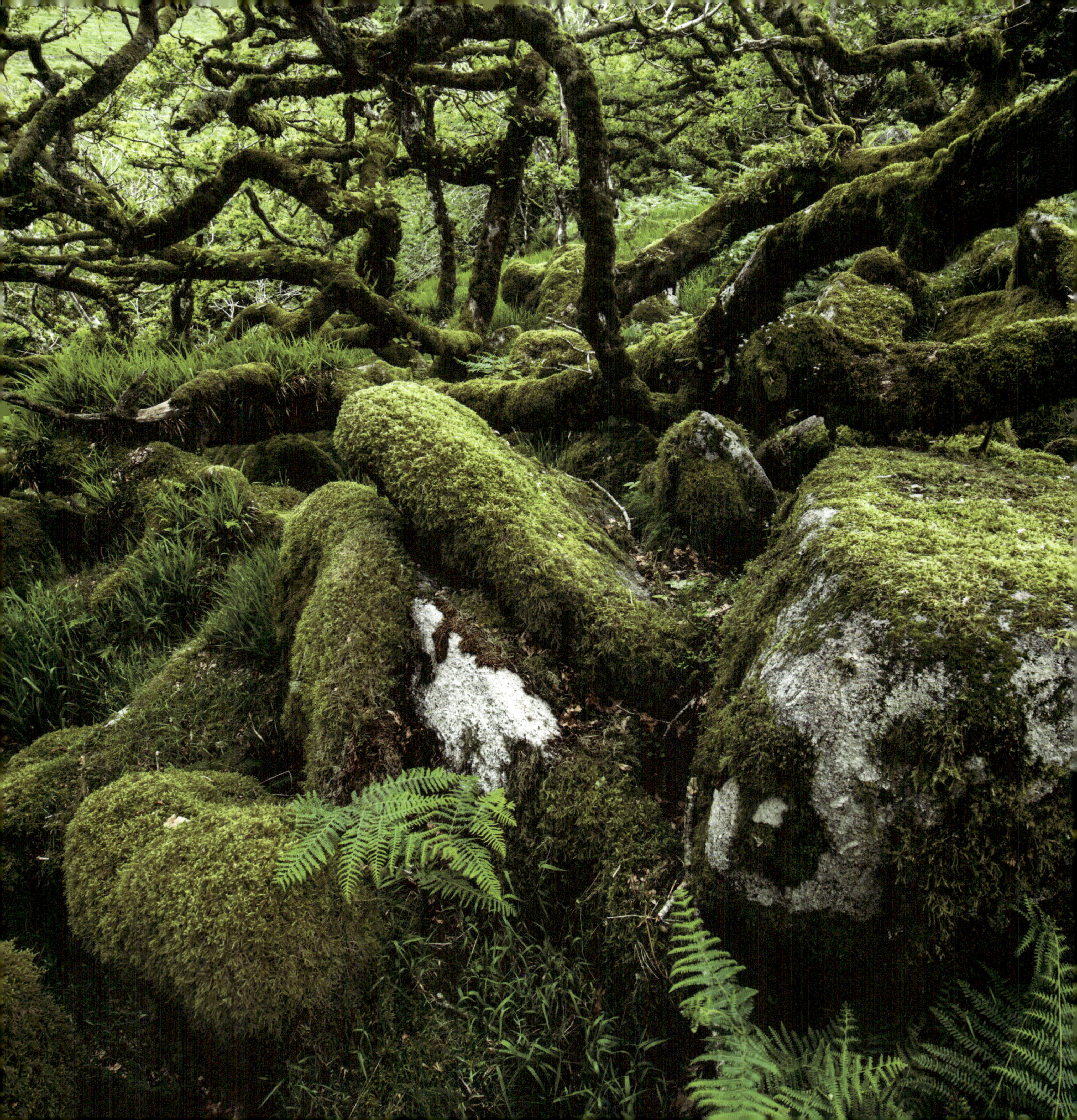

The Beatles were one of the first bands to write and record their own material …

The austere conditions which had prevailed into '50s Britain – food rationing and a general feeling of dowdiness and poverty – gradually receded as the country began to recover its prosperity. By the beginning of the '60s a new generation was growing up, free to live their teenage years uninterrupted by National Service. Within the working classes jobs were there to be had; there were apprenticeship schemes and casual labour could always be found.

For years the middle classes alone had been able to send their children through grammar school and then on to university, but this exclusivity was slipping; now working-class children could follow the same route. A new strand of young people emerged, better educated and with wider expectations of life from a far earlier age than their parents.

At the beginning of the '60s a new pop group appeared from Liverpool. The Beatles were one of the first bands to write and record their own material, even though their early songs, while musically clever and catchy, relied heavily on the boy-meets-girl cliché. This, though, was to change later on.

The early '60s pop scene in Liverpool produced a whole series of groups who set about following The Beatles' example and the explosion known as the 'Merseybeat' was born. By clever manipulation of the media The Beatles' manager, Brian Epstein, created a massive market for the group and by the mid-'60s they were the most successful recording act since Elvis Presley.

Back in London a new musical movement had taken root. Having been the passing craze that everyone had predicted it would be, skiffle was now on the decline, but many skiffle musicians were graduating to a musically more sophisticated influence – the blues.

Blues records had found their way into England through the docks of Liverpool and London, introduced by merchant seamen who had spent time in America, had heard the music and been able to buy it in American shops. Soon a number of specialist record shops began to stock blues music and blues awareness began to develop amongst those in the know.

A blues club scene was established in London by a number of these ex-skiffle musicians. Two of them, Alexis Korner and Cyril Davies, formed a club called The Roundhouse, in a pub in the West End. Korner subsequently broke away and formed his own club at Ealing in West London, called, appropriately enough, The Ealing Club.

The music which Alexis Korner and Cyril Davies were playing at their respective clubs was hard-driving, Chicago blues – far removed from anything so trivial as pop music. Indeed, its followers displayed a growing antagonism towards the clean-cut image and suits of bands like The Beatles. The scene was therefore perfectly set for a new group to come along and exist in opposition to The Beatles' nice boy image.

Dylan's lyrics were unlike anything anyone had heard before; they were articulate and full of social commentary.

In due course The Rolling Stones emerged from this club scene. Rebellious and irreverent, they showed no respect for the class values of the time, even subjugating their own middle-class accents in favour of a pseudo-cockney dialect. With the floodgates opened, dozens of rhythm and blues bands – The Animals and The Pretty Things, for example – came to prominence soon afterwards.

During the '60s only a small number of record labels operated in England, all of them large corporations, or what we now refer to as 'majors'. Among the largest were EMI and Decca; The Beatles had signed to EMI and so, not surprisingly, The Rolling Stones went to Decca.

Slowly the lyrical content of pop songs began to change as a new generation of writers – among them The Kinks' Ray Davies and Pete Townshend of The Who – started to express more sophisticated ideas through their music. In America a similar transition was taking place and one man, almost single-handedly, changed both the public's and the media's perception of youth music as an art form. His name was Bob Dylan.

Dylan had grown up in a middle-class Jewish family in Minnesota and had invented a mythology around his own life. This mythology he took with him to the folk club scene in Boston and New York, where folk artists performed their songs in coffee houses, to audiences who were keen to listen to the new message. Dylan's lyrics were unlike anything anyone had heard before; they were articulate and full of social commentary.

The USA's involvement in the Vietnam War at this time meant that fresh generations of young Americans were growing up with service in Vietnam a distinct possibility. Students at American universities were quick to organise a protest movement against the war, with rallies, marches, sit-ins and the burning of draft cards.

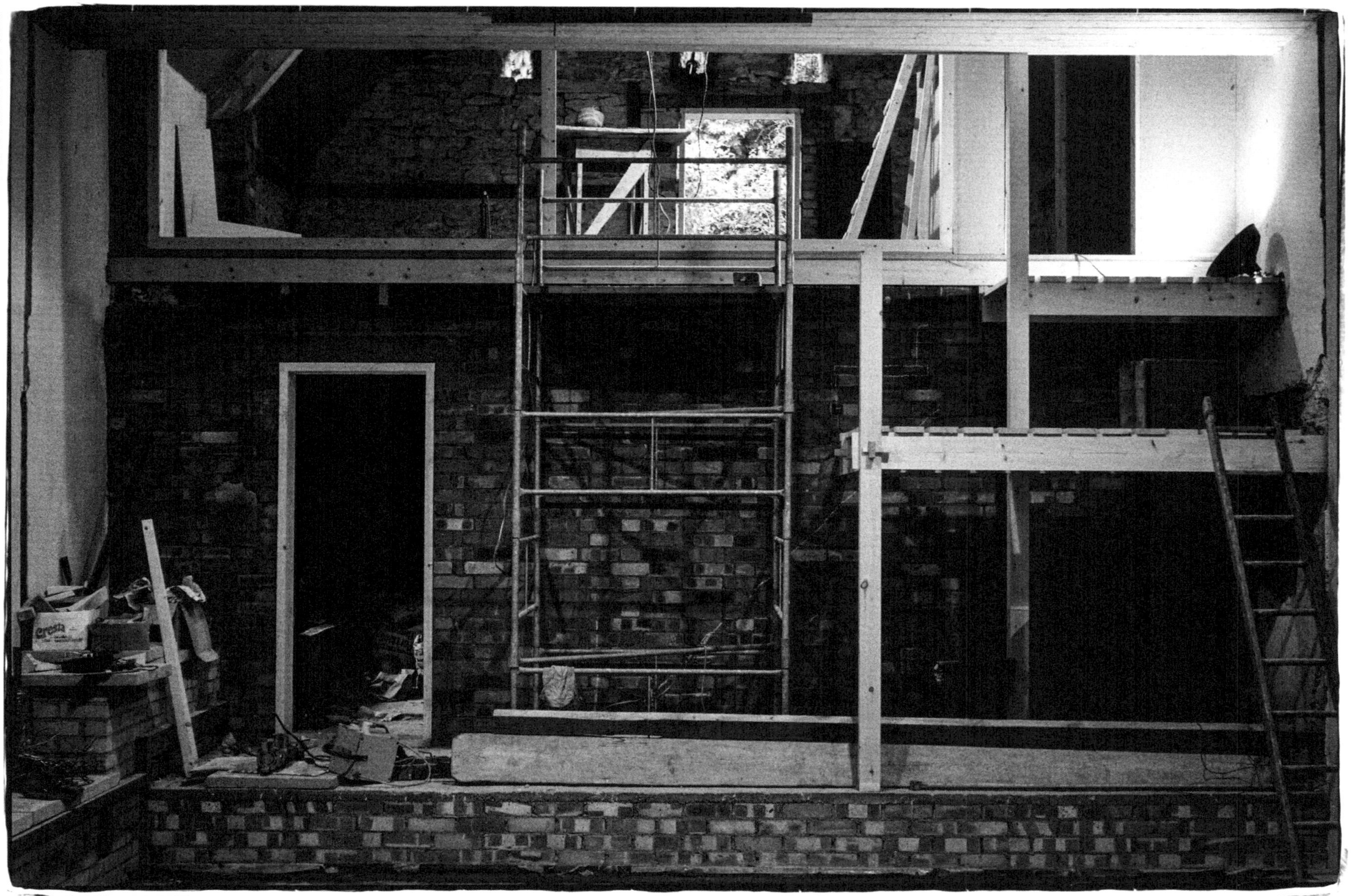

PHOTO: SIMON HEYWORTH

The studio takes shape

'Sgt. Pepper's Lonely Hearts Club Band' broke all grounds ... the production of the record showed a sophistication never before seen ...

Back in England the '60s generation began to realise that something was happening to their American contemporaries. As television developed as a news medium, pictures from the Vietnam War and the protest movement against it were regularly shown to the British public. These were to have a profound effect on the student population of Great Britain, particularly in London.

So the climate was changing, not only in America and Great Britain, but also throughout Europe. Pre-war middle-class values were being challenged by a more affluent generation with a very different outlook on life from that of their parents.

Meanwhile, many of the groups who had signed record contracts and released pop records during the early to mid-'60s were finding that, as they grew older, their audience remained. For the first time, the prospect of a long-term career in pop music became a reality. As both artist and audience grew older, they were reluctant to give up the culture of the music which had become so important to them.

As Bob Dylan's records found their way to England, other artists followed his example of writing songs about more weighty subjects in life than the boy-meets-girl scenario. All these musical and social pressures were to come together in 1967 in what is remembered as the beginning of the psychedelic years; The Velvet Opera, Procol Harum, Pink Floyd, Traffic and even Cream were in the vanguard with this 'underground' music.

The Rolling Stones and The Beatles were also growing up and finding that, far from being a short-lived phenomenon, their musical careers were stretching onwards. Influenced by much of the music that was coming out of America, The Beatles had been changing style and writing more complex songs about more complex subjects. In fact, by the time of psychedelia they were world leaders in music, not only lyrically, but also in their use of studio-created sounds and – against the general grain of pop music – orchestral arrangements.

These elements, aided by some experimentation with drugs such as cannabis and LSD, combined to create an album which was to change the world's perception of pop music forever.

'Sgt. Pepper's Lonely Hearts Club Band' broke all grounds: the record's cover was designed by an established British pop artist, called Peter Blake; the lyrics were anything but the average pop fare; and the production of the record showed a sophistication never before seen, courtesy of a staff producer at EMI Records named George Martin.

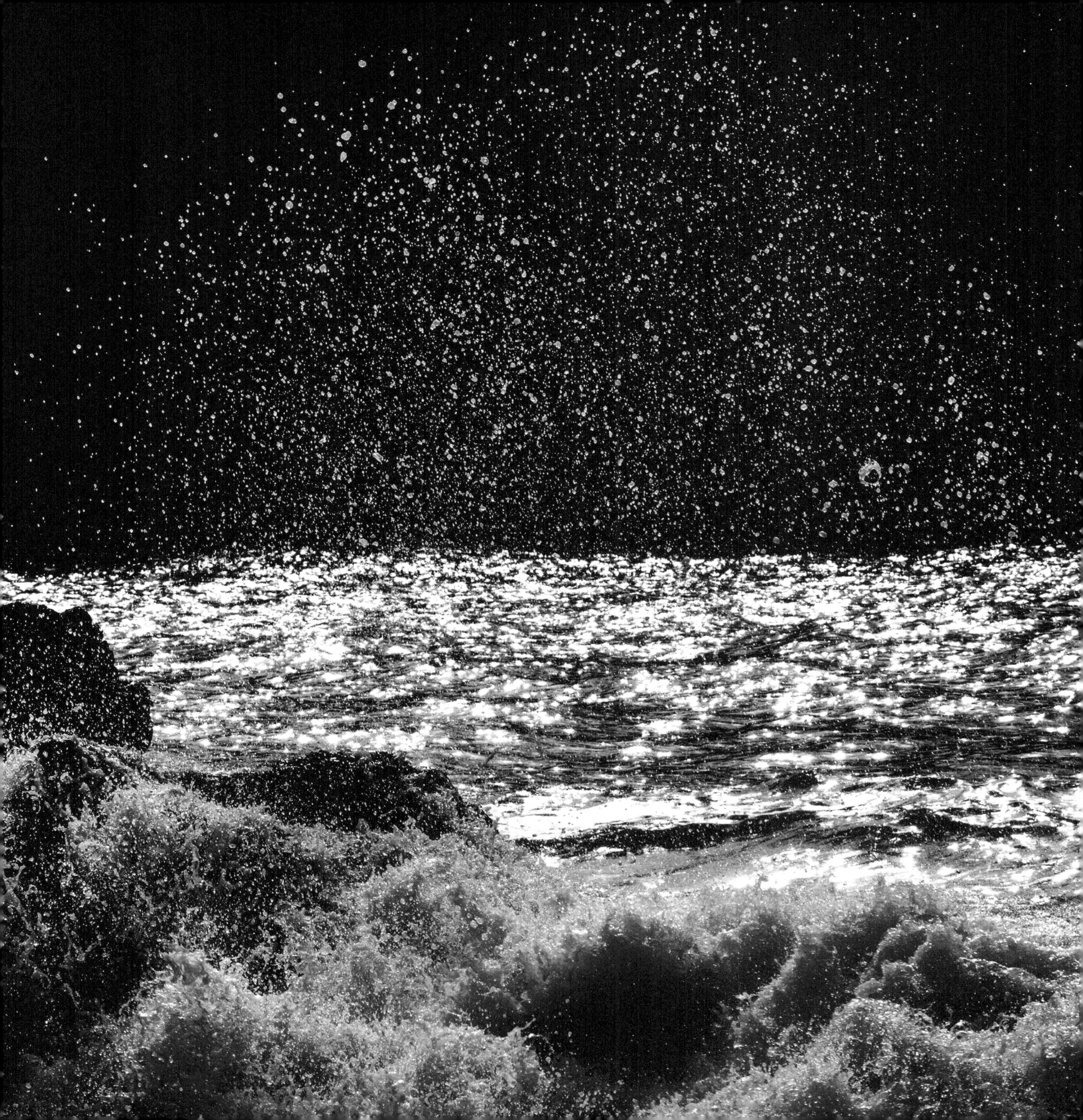

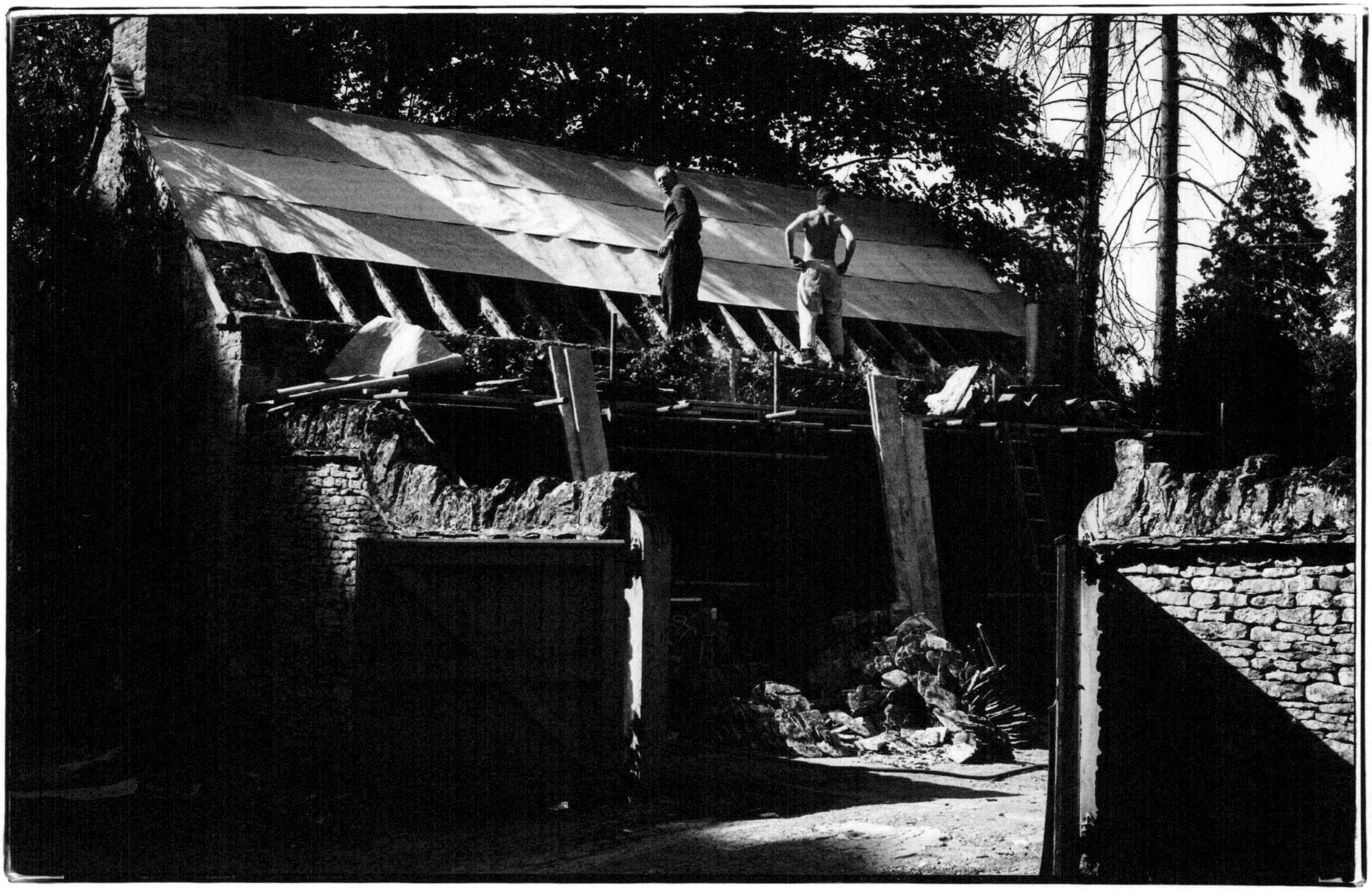

PHOTO: SIMON HEYWORTH

Tom Newman: "It was a little stable with a hayloft above, which I converted into the control room"

A natural practical joker, the boy had, like many others of his generation, a talent for creating a mythology about himself and his life. His name was Richard Branson.

The release of 'Sgt. Pepper ...' gave the youth culture of the day a piece of work behind which to unify. The British media also began to engage with the art form that was the product of this young energy. In late 1967 and early 1968 the term 'rock music' began to be used to distinguish this type of 'serious' music from pop.

Pop music meanwhile was carrying on in its normal way, producing new young bands who released singles and tried to gain entry to the pop charts.

A number of television programmes also tried to cater to this youth market. One such programme was to be very influential as it covered the new rock music, as well as including the existing pop scene. 'Ready Steady Go!' was broadcast on Friday evenings from television studios in London's Kingsway. It was to reflect changes in fashion and in dance crazes, as well as providing a stage for such bands as Cream – part of the emerging counter-culture.

So momentum was gathering in a number of areas. Pop was becoming more sophisticated and the younger generation – the student population in particular – was feeling a new freedom to express itself. This expression could be readily seen in the long hair and colourful 'hippy' fashions of the time, but there were underlying changes, too, such as experimentation with drugs and a sexual freedom aided and abetted by the introduction of the birth control pill.

By the end of the '60s the youth movement had its own rock bands and its own culture. However, some people were also beginning to realise that such a body of people represented a significant marketplace.

At around this time a pupil at an English public school had become interested in the student movement. This boy found himself increasingly at odds with a system which demanded adherence to a moral code and ethical outlook openly challenged outside the public school domain. A natural practical joker, the boy had, like many others of his generation, a talent for creating a mythology about himself and his life. His name was Richard Branson.

While at Stowe public school he had organised a student protest against conditions there, amazing colleagues with his unquenchable energy and an attitude that declared anything was possible. After convincing his parents that he did not wish to follow the accepted route to university, Branson eventually left Stowe to take over a property that had been temporarily leased by them in Albion Street, London.

From this temporary accommodation Richard Branson was to form 'Student' magazine, rapidly recruiting all sorts of counter-culture people as well as students and people looking for a quick way to make small amounts of money.

Totally absorbed and with a great love of classical music, Oldfield began to fuse a number of different styles into his compositions. He soon decided that he would like to become a professional musician and so took up the electric guitar and also the electric bass guitar.

'Student' magazine was created and distributed by what rapidly turned into a community centred on Albion Street. The whole thing was disorganised and unprofessional, but the people working on the magazine and distributing it believed in what they were doing. Most importantly, Richard Branson was able to motivate them and inspire them to work for next to nothing.

Not surprisingly, the operation became a magnet for all kinds of people. Some were idealists and some were simply trying to exploit the situation for their own ends. But it was becoming clear, especially to Branson, that although the idealism that had supported the Summer of Love was becoming increasingly tarnished by events, the people involved in the new movement were still prepared to buy records. This allowed them to withdraw from active involvement while still maintaining a link with the culture.

It was to this market that 'Student' magazine attempted to sell.

During the whole of this period the major record labels – EMI, Decca and Philips etc. – had dominated the record-making scene in England. One young man was to break that mould.

Chris Blackwell had also been to public school and had seen the possibilities of making money by selling records to this enthusiastic generation of young people. In response he formed Island Records, a label which rapidly established itself as the first 'independent' of any significance.

From initially just issuing Jamaican reggae records, Island expanded its musical policy; the way was clear for some of the new rock groups to be signed, most notably a band called Free.

As time progressed, the rock culture, as expressed through records, began to draw in new generations of young people who, when they were tired of the banal nature of pop music, graduated to this 'more serious' art form.

At the same time, there was a dramatic increase in the virtuosity of musicians playing the new music – itself a crucial factor in the success of 'Tubular Bells'. Pop groups would stand onstage, look cute and strum a few chords on the guitar. With a catchy verse and a singalong chorus a band stood every chance, with the right exposure and media manipulation, of having a hit record. But to be part of the rock band culture, some degree of skill with your instrument was necessary.

By the late '60s, a whole set of British guitar players had become world-famous for such displays of ability. Eric Clapton, Peter Green, Jimmy Page and Jeff Beck had earned reputations as articulate and sophisticated musicians, as respected by other players as by the public at large.

From the start, Oldfield displayed an extraordinary gift as a musician and by the time he was 14 he was already an accomplished player.

With all this going on, another musical movement had been taking place in England. In the wake of Bob Dylan's considerable influence, the folk club scene had grown in strength. Dylan, accompanying himself on an acoustic guitar like his hero, American folk singer-songwriter Woody Guthrie, inspired a new trend. All over Great Britain young people were buying acoustic guitars, learning a few chords and joining in with this movement.

Of course, there had always been a British folk scene. Indeed, traditional 'folkies' were often the subject of ridicule. They would sing traditional songs from England, Scotland, Ireland and Wales, totally unaccompanied, often with a finger in one ear so that they could hear their voices better. Thus was born the image of the trad folkie that was the cause of such mirth to outsiders.

But a new form of folk club began to appear – what became known as contemporary folk clubs – where you could hear the new singer-songwriters. British musicians such as Ralph McTell and Al Stewart could be heard exploring the same music as their American contemporaries, fine musicians such as Paul Simon and James Taylor.

Within the folk music scene a small number of musicians were displaying a singular virtuosity on the guitar. Among the older generation two were notable: Wizz Jones and Davey Graham. They, in turn, were to influence many younger players. Bert Jansch and John Renbourn were two such inspired players, composing instrumental pieces of their own on the guitar. Transatlantic Records, an independent folk record label which had been formed to cater for this new music, signed both men.

During this period, a young man was growing up in Reading, Berkshire. Family difficulties made home life unhappy and, like many others, music offered an escape from the day-to-day problems of life. His sister had developed an interest in folk music, singing at local folk clubs, and one day she brought home a new boyfriend and his acoustic guitar. Eventually the new boyfriend was encouraged to play and the effect on the young man watching was profound. He knew that he had to learn to play this instrument. His name was Mike Oldfield.

Eventually Mike Oldfield was to join forces as a musical duo with his sister. The Sallyangie made two records for the new folk label Transatlantic.

From the start, Oldfield displayed an extraordinary gift as a musician and by the time he was 14 he was already an accomplished player. Influenced by the playing of Bert Jansch and John Renbourn he spent many hours analysing their records, learning their instrumental compositions until eventually he began to write his own music on the guitar.

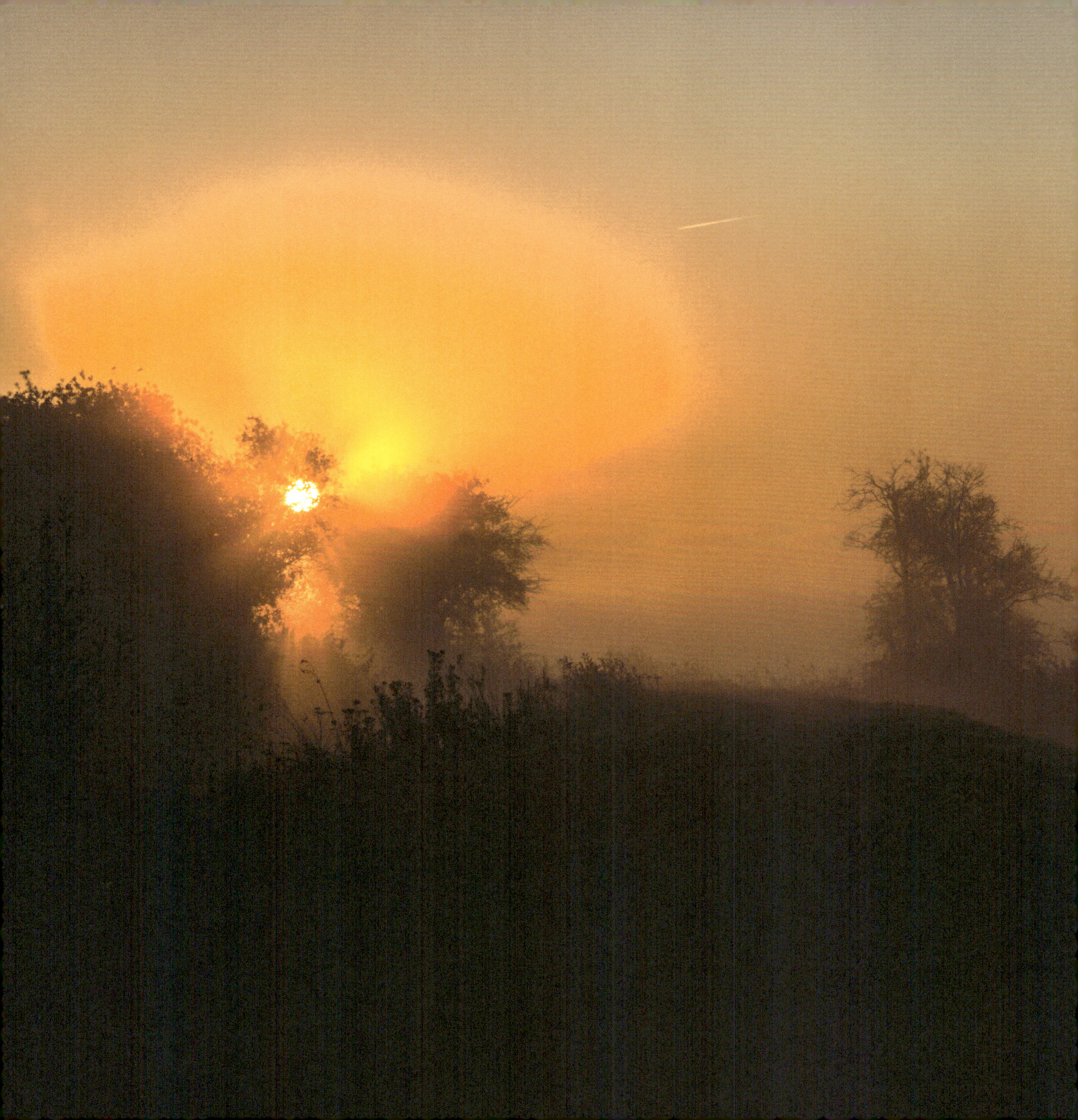

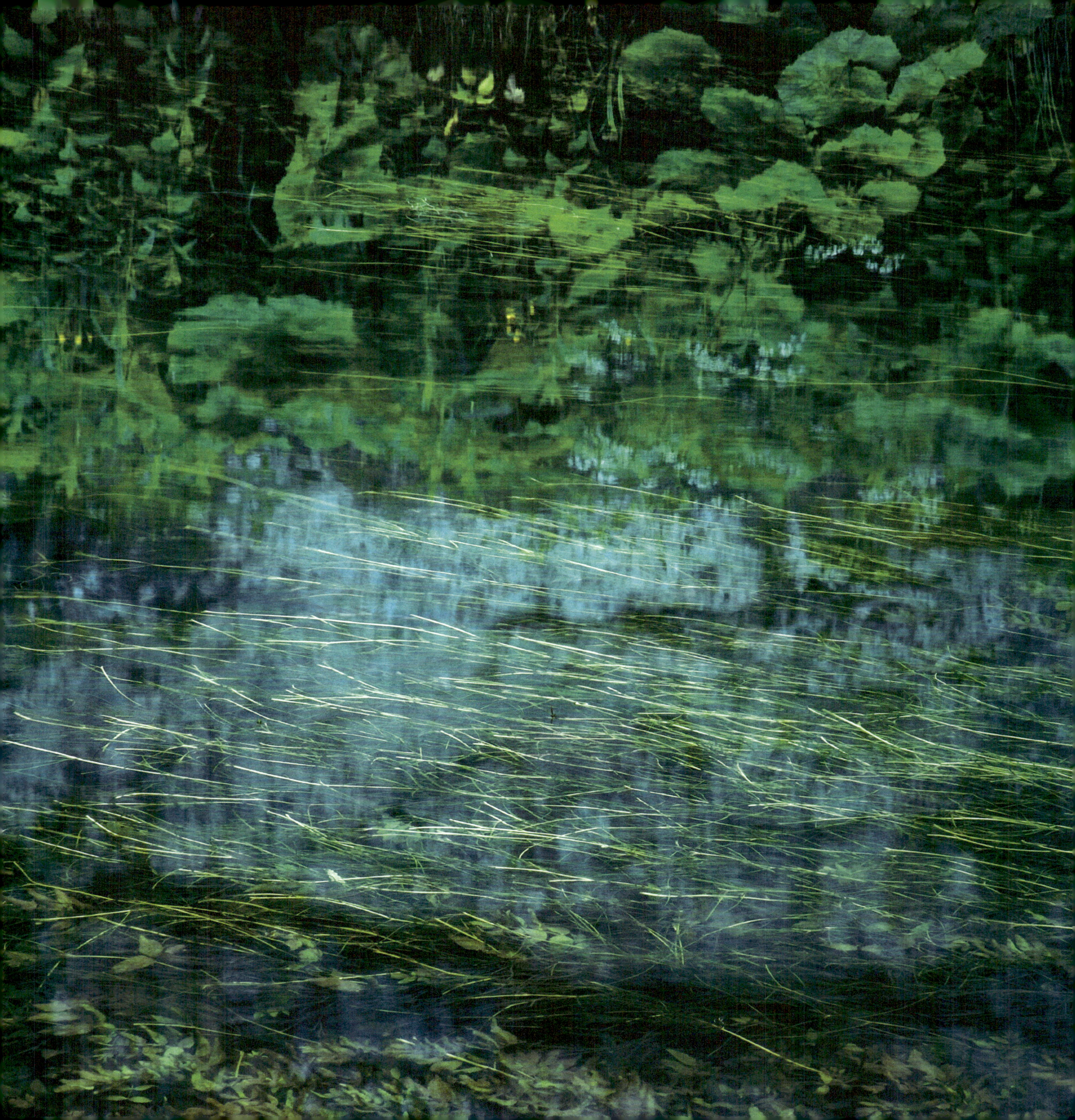

Totally absorbed and with a great love of classical music, Oldfield began to fuse a number of different styles into his compositions. He soon decided that he would like to become a professional musician and so took up the electric guitar and also the electric bass guitar.

The Sallyangie eventually came to an end and Mike joined Kevin Ayers – a founder member of Soft Machine, a famous underground rock band of the '60s – in a new group called Kevin Ayers & The Whole World. Oldfield played bass guitar and electric lead guitar and soon gained a similar reputation for his electric playing as he had done when playing the acoustic guitar at local folk clubs. Following a split with Kevin Ayers,` he ended up as a bass player in a band run by a man called Arthur Lewis, playing music which was a cross between the styles of Jimi Hendrix and Bob Dylan.

Not happy in this group, Oldfield was still trying to make his way as a professional musician and was now beginning to suffer from severe stress brought on by the disintegration of his home life.

But Arthur Lewis had decided it was time to put some of the music of the group onto tape as a 'demo' – a demonstration tape which a band would play to a record company in the hope of securing a contract. Lewis ended up making this demo at a new kind of recording studio which was still in the process of being built, in the stables of an old country house in Oxfordshire.

This studio was called The Manor. Owned by Richard Branson, it was being built by two young men – Tom Newman assisted by Simon Heyworth.

Simon Heyworth was from a middle-class background and had been to public school before going to America to continue his studies. Whilst studying on an English-speaking scholarship in Claremont, near Pasadena in California, Heyworth attended concerts by such bands as Buffalo Springfield, The Grateful Dead and The Jimi Hendrix Experience.

At the age of 18 he returned to England and took up his studies at the London Academy of Music and Dramatic Art, known worldwide by its initials LAMDA. Simon's course involved stage management and production, but he was also very interested in sound and was developing something of a passion for film. After one and a half years Simon decided that stage management within the theatre was not for him and he left LAMDA.

During his time as a student Simon had become friendly with someone from Tangerine Recording Studios and had been along to watch some sessions. He became fascinated by the process of recording and made up his mind to become a recording engineer. Consequently, he was on the lookout for opportunities to break into the recording studio scene when he heard about a strange operation going on in South Wharf Road in London – a student help organisation and a mail order record label called Caroline Records.

'Tubular Bells' was to be the first piece of music released on Richard Branson's record label ...

Heyworth paid a visit to South Wharf Road and there he met Tom Newman, someone with an equal interest in sound recording. Caroline Records and the helpline were being run by the young entrepreneur, Richard Branson.

Tom Newman immediately took to Simon Heyworth and told him about the new studio that he was going to build for Branson. To Simon Heyworth this was the golden opportunity to break into the studio scene. Newman was so taken by Simon's positive attitude and enthusiasm that he immediately asked him to become part of the team that was to build The Manor.

So, whether by coincidence or fate, all the main players were in place. As we have seen, a market existed for the new rock music, a market which was growing by the week and was hungry for new products. The result of the meetings of Richard Branson and Tom Newman and subsequently of Tom Newman, Simon Heyworth and then Mike Oldfield, was to be a piece of music which would be taken to heart by the new rock music generation. The stage for 'Tubular Bells' was set.

'Tubular Bells' was to be the first piece of music released on Richard Branson's record label – his next big idea after the collapse of 'Student' magazine. In trying to think of a name for his new label, Branson decided on Virgin because, legend has it, no one involved had had any experience of running a record label.

The subsequent success of 'Tubular Bells' provided the initial finance that allowed Branson to expand Virgin Records into the force that it became and which, in turn, became the basis for the formation of Virgin Airlines.

the manor

- 16/8/14-track studio
- 60 minutes from London
- 100-acre grounds
- Resident engineers
- Resident cooks
- Room for producers, wives, girlfriends, roadies
- Day and night recording
- Free food and beds
- Good rates, etc.
- 16-track Ampex
- 20-channel desk
- Equalisation
- Dolby noise reduction
- Quadrophonic monitoring
- Phasing facilities
- Echo facilities: tapes/plates/springs/drums
- Grand piano
- Room for 40 musicians, etc.

Specification of The Manor; the first residential recording studio in the UK

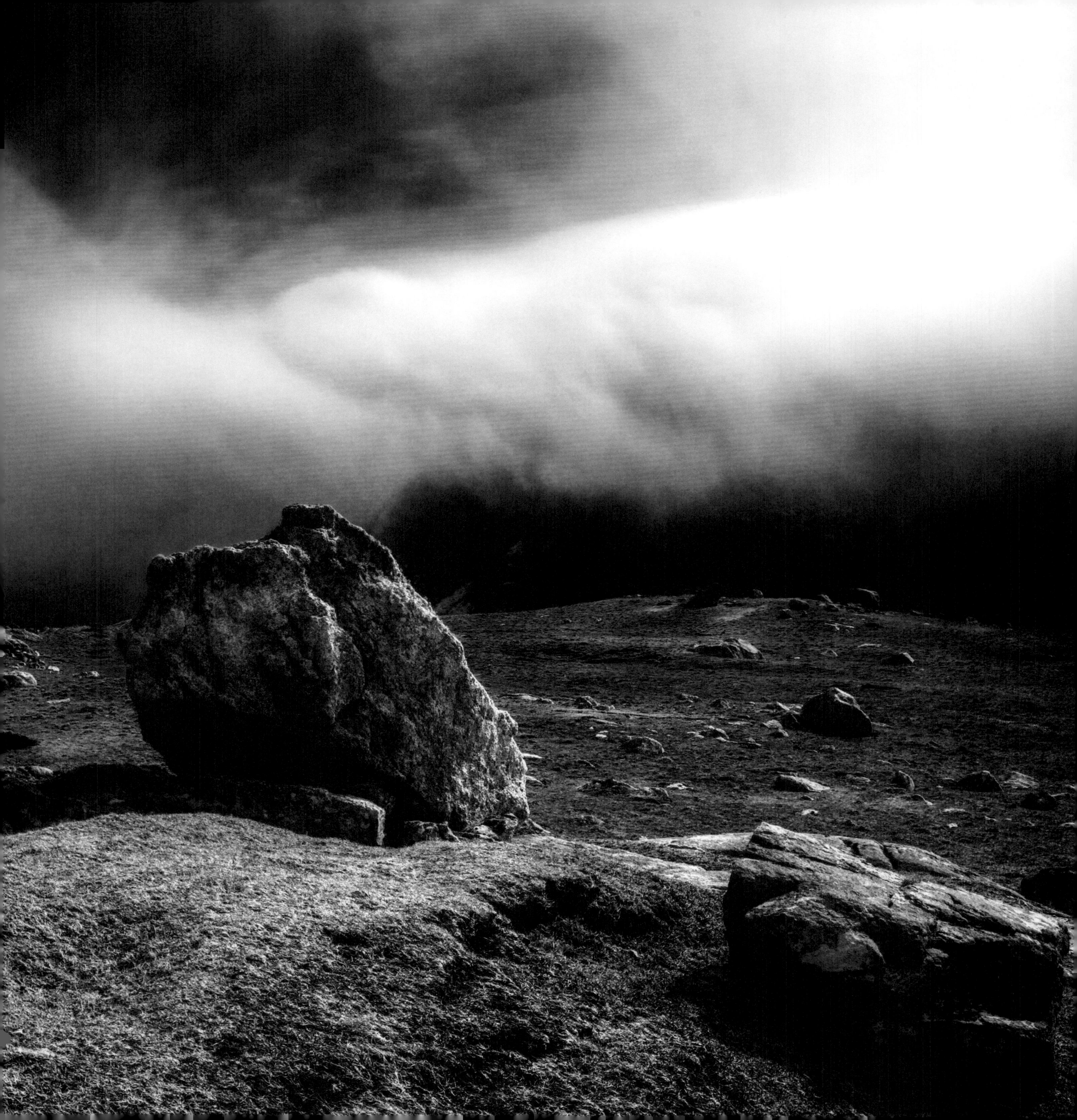

2

VIRGIN RECORDS AND THE BUILDING OF THE MANOR RECORDING STUDIO

THIS is the story of how a 19-year-old called Mike Oldfield made an album which went on to sell over 15,000,000 copies worldwide and is still selling more than 100,000 copies a year. The story encapsulates the early days of what was to become a powerful business empire and details the building of the first residential country recording studio. Mike Oldfield recalls the initial tentative steps ...

Mike Oldfield: "I remember I had completely given up hope. I had taken these tapes round to the record companies who looked at me as if I was mad. They all said that because there were no vocals, no words, no drums or anything, that it was not marketable. I later found out that that means it would not sell, that no one would buy it."

The credits on 'Tubular Bells' tell us that two other people were involved in getting the music onto tape. They were Tom Newman and Simon Heyworth.

Having talked Richard Branson into the idea, Newman, with the aid of Simon Heyworth, was in the process of building The Manor studio. But it was taking a long time to finish and, in desperation, Branson sent down a band for a recording session, as a way of putting pressure on Tom and his team to get things working.

The band was called The Arthur Lewis Band and one of the members of the band was Mike Oldfield.

PHOTO: SIMON HEYWORTH

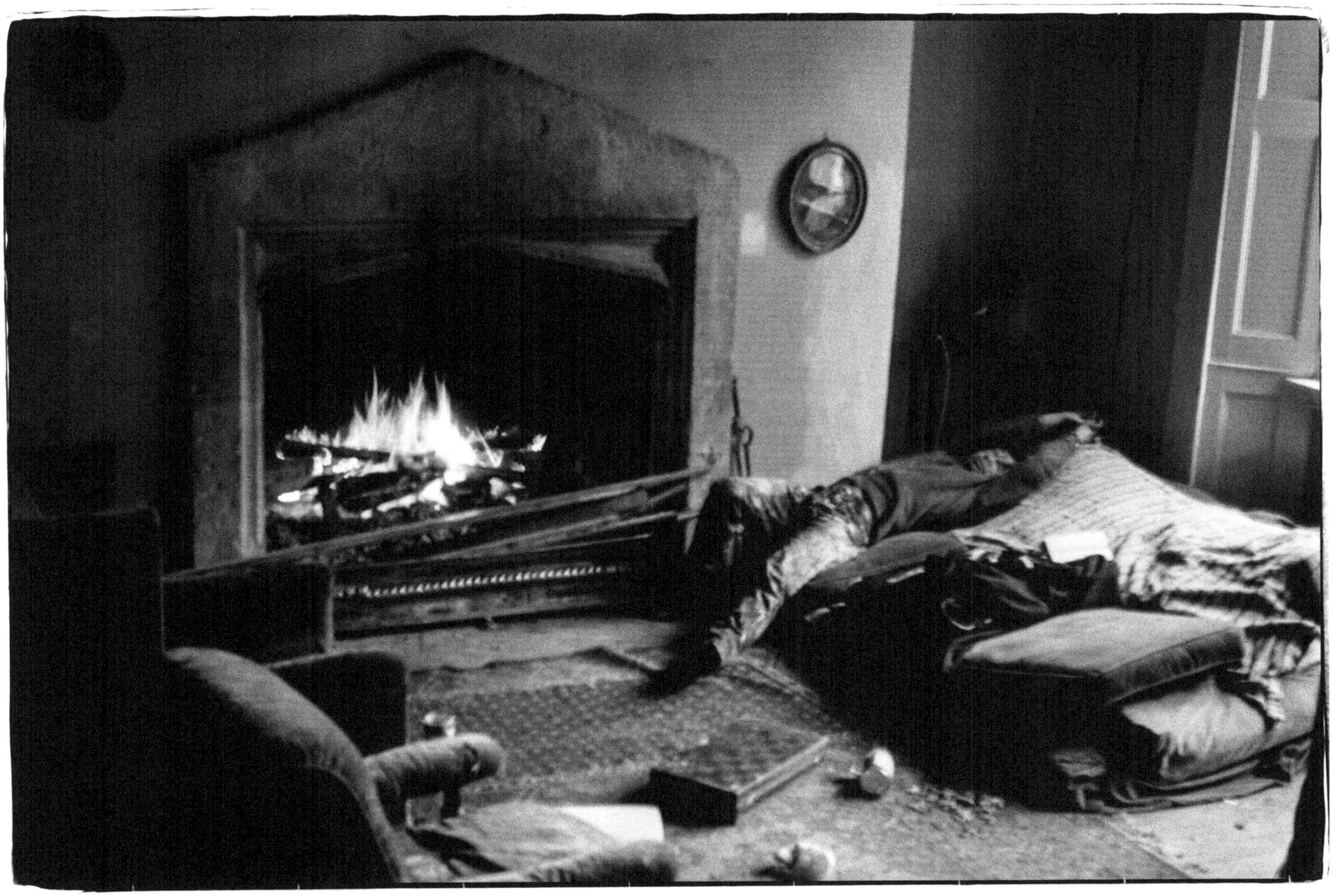

Mike Oldfield: "It was a wonderful place. The Manor; it was a big old stone house with a lovely great big fireplace and the whole atmosphere there was really exciting."

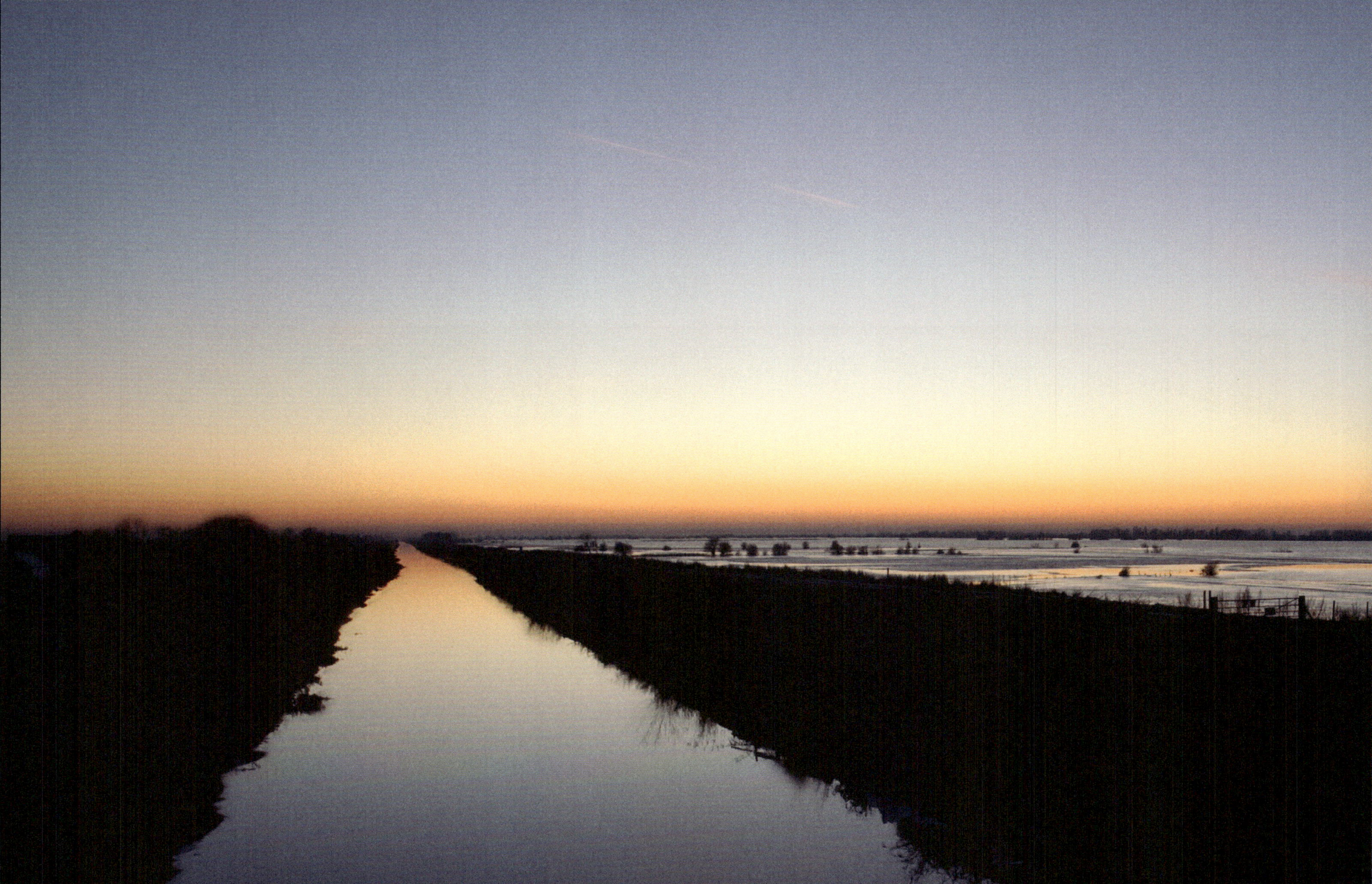

"To practise with a whole band takes a lot of organisation. With an acoustic guitar you just pick it up and sit in your bedroom and play the night away if you want." MIKE OLDFIELD

Tom Newman: "I was sitting at the mixer, prodding and fiddling, and Michael's face appeared and he said, 'Simon says you are the boss!', and I said, 'Yeah, what's the matter?' He had invaded my space and I thought that maybe he was drunk or something.

"He said: 'Listen to this,' and poked this little tape at me. I said, 'What is it?' and he said, 'It's me; it's really, really good.' And I believed him, though I thought he was mad. So I said, 'All right, I'll listen to it later, now go away!'

"A few days later he came up to me again and said, 'Have you listened to it yet?' and I said, 'Oh no, sorry, I forgot.' But I had an old tape machine in my room, which was in the loft, so I went up and put the tape on. I was completely spellbound and I was there four or five hours, playing Michael's tape over and over."

This tape was a rough demo that Oldfield had been painstakingly putting together. He had recently given the music a name: 'Tubular Bells'.

Mike Oldfield was a fine acoustic guitarist. He had formulated various extended pieces of music which he had been performing at folk clubs and these can be viewed as the germs that were to grow into 'Tubular Bells'.

Mike Oldfield: "One day my sister Sally came home with a new boyfriend and I remember he got out this acoustic guitar and suddenly he was playing. I couldn't believe it! I just made up my mind that I'd got to be able to do that. Sally was interested in folk music and I went along to a folk club with her and there were people playing acoustic music really well. People like Bert Jansch and John Renbourn were around at that time and I would buy their records and spend the whole weekend working out how to play their instruments. That was lucky because it gave me many good techniques and then I could start making up my own.

"I used to have two, 15-minute instrumentals which I'd play at folk clubs, during which I would go through all sorts of moods. I even did bits of detuning the strings totally and all sorts of stuff. I spent all my time playing guitar. The minute I came home from school the entire weekend would be spent practising and playing guitar. I studied and I was getting a really good response from people. I was even offered a residency at a local Reading folk club.

"I found this was something which I could really be appreciated for – in the electric bands I'd had, which tended to be at the local village hall dance, people would not be so appreciative, whereas I could go to a folk club and play one of my instruments and get a very good response.

"My listening started with Lonnie Donegan singing a song called 'Love Is Strange'." TOM NEWMAN

Also I didn't make a lot of noise at home. To practise with a whole band takes a lot of organisation. With an acoustic guitar you just pick it up and sit in your bedroom and play the night away if you want. There was nothing to hurt anybody.

"So I developed my technique and began to make up instrumentals, and in a way these became a sort of skeleton blueprint for what was to become 'Tubular Bells'. That's not to say that I used to play the whole thing on acoustic guitar, but there were little elements of it and the way it was structured; I learned how to dovetail one section of music into another."

Meanwhile, Tom Newman was having a very different musical education.

Tom Newman: "For me, The Beatles were the big thing. I mean, 'Sgt. Pepper ...' was my Bible, I was soaking it up and it was a seminal thing for me.

"My listening started with Lonnie Donegan singing a song called 'Love Is Strange'. It's got this little guitar lick that's all distant and swimmy and a long way away, but his voice is right up in your face. It was actually produced by Joe Meek, a wonderful, wonderful track, totally empty and very poetically strong for me."

Tom Newman had been an only child and had grown up living on a converted landing craft that was moored on the River Thames at Richmond in Surrey. He lived in a world of his own and would act out boyhood fantasies on a deserted island near to where his father's boat was moored. His early experience of music fuelled a vivid imagination and a love of songs such as Frankie Laine's 'Ghost Riders in the Sky', the lyrics of which painted pictures in his mind.

After leaving school he formed a skiffle band, The Playboys, and then a blues band called The Tomcats. Although The Tomcats played blues Newman was able to see past the English pastiche.

Tom Newman: "The Blues is a genuine tearing open of your chest with an ethnic minority in a racially insupportable situation. In America at that time it was a nightmare for those people. It was real for them and we didn't know that. It wasn't a nightmare for us, we were just on to a fast buck. We were doing the blues because we wanted to be famous and have a lot of money. We thought that we understood it, but we didn't, we couldn't have done. It was nonsense. We didn't know about the Devil at the crossroads in the same way as Robert Johnson did. He believed it, we believed in Jesus and Christmas, we didn't believe in the Devil. We didn't go to the crossroads and say, 'Take me'; that was too frightening to even consider."

PHOTO: SIMON HEYWORTH

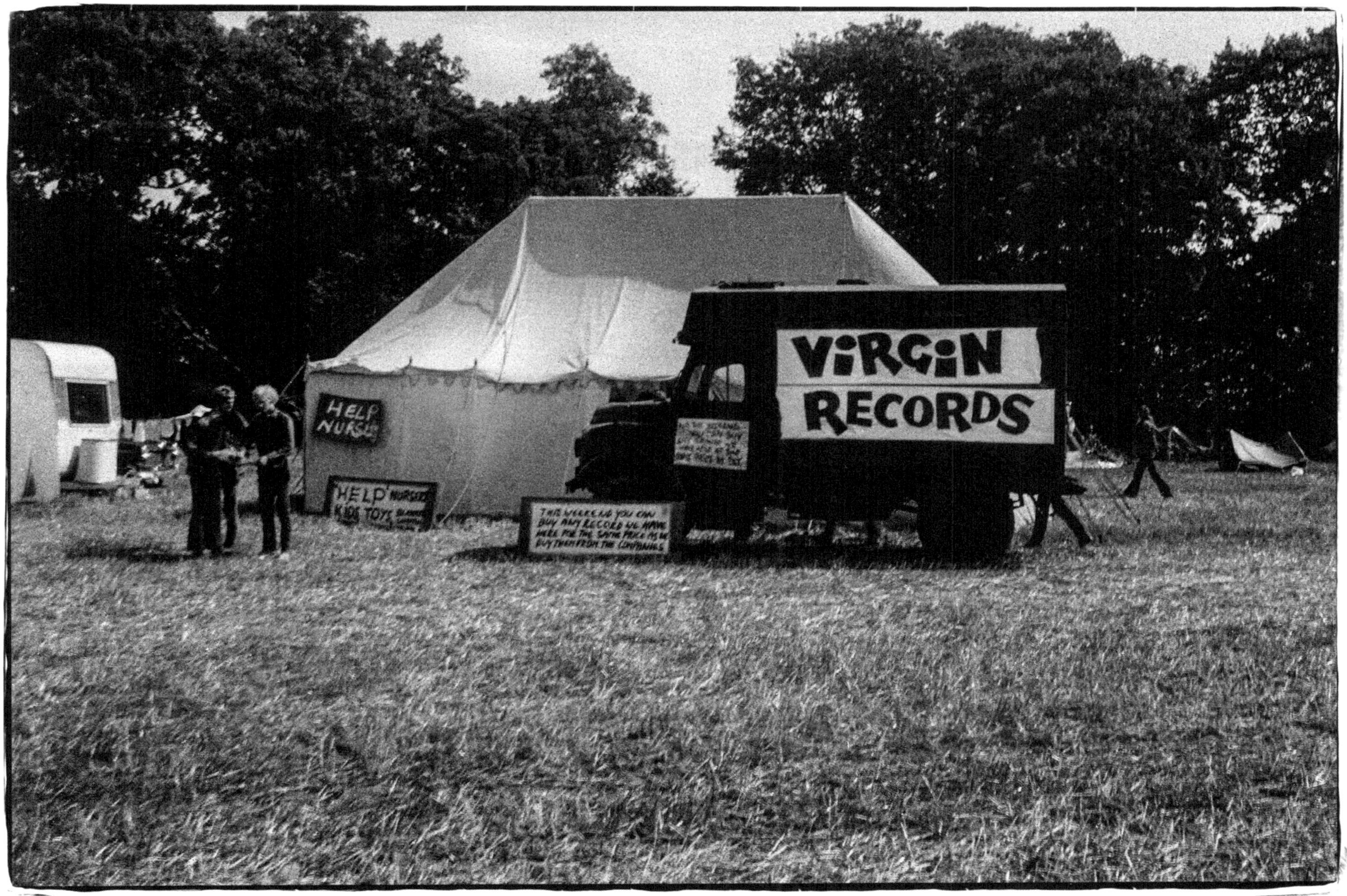

From little acorns … Richard Branson was later to sell 'this' for £560,000,000!

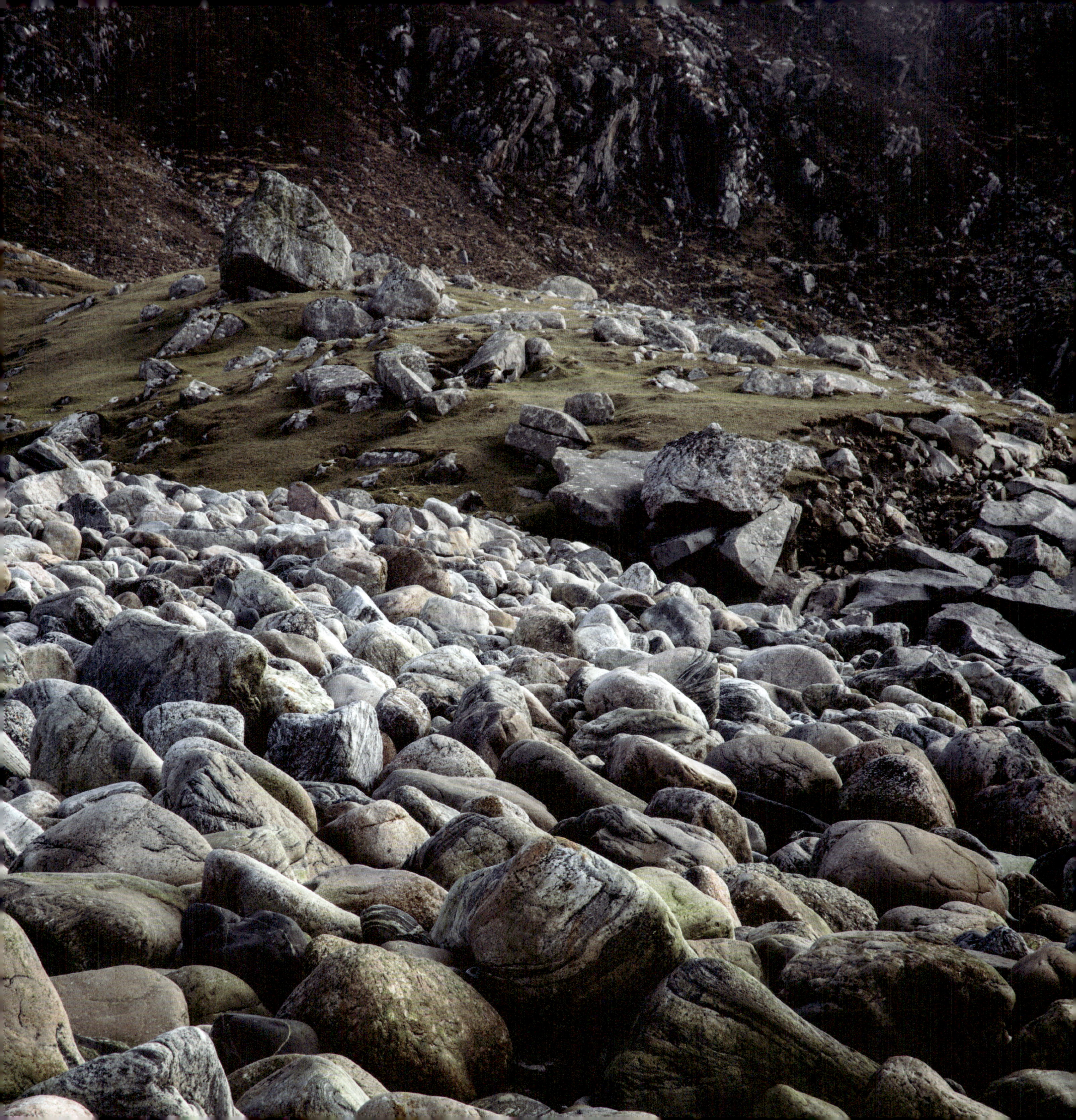

This 'strange guy' ... ran a student help organisation and sold mail order records. His name, of course, was Richard Branson.

The young English blues guitarist Peter Green had formed his own band, Fleetwood Mac. One of Green's compositions was an instrumental called 'Albatross'.

Tom Newman: "Green has this real strange character. There were bits of what Fleetwood Mac did in their early days that really touched me. 'Albatross' was an amazing piece of work for the period, another seminal work for me; I was really deeply affected by it. If you go up to the ice floes in the Arctic they all look the same, but occasionally you get a really strange one, one that sticks up above the rest. 'Albatross' was like that for me; it leapt out and grabbed you and dragged you back into place with it. It was pictures in the mind again, because it was so different. There were one or two tracks like that, that just leapt out."

After The Tomcats, Tom Newman formed a psychedelic band called July, who signed a record contract with a label called Major Minor. Eventually the band broke up but during this period, Newman had started to experiment with recording sound. He was out of a band but was still writing songs and was keen to commit them to tape in the form of rough demos. What he really wanted to do was to set up a small demo studio.

One day he went to pick up his girlfriend from work. Her name was Jackie Byford and occasionally she worked for this 'strange guy' in Albion Street who was running a student magazine. This 'strange guy' was the same young man who also had premises in South Wharf Road, from where he ran a student help organisation and sold mail order records. His name, of course, was Richard Branson.

Tom Newman: "Jackie Byford worked occasionally for this guy in Albion Street and he was running a magazine called 'Student' magazine. My band, July, actually had a record deal but then the record company folded right on the cusp of us doing the Albert Hall! We were doing very well and we were getting a good following and then the record company collapsed. And then the management company collapsed. And then all the equipment got taken back because the whole thing had fallen apart.

"So I found myself out on my own but I still had a lot of songs that I had half done. I wanted to carry on and record my songs and maybe start a new band or maybe go solo. I was in a state of flux really, because the band had been my whole life for seven or eight years and I was suddenly out in the great big world by myself, without help.

"My mum and dad had left and gone to Ireland and I was living in the back of my van. I then moved in with Jackie Byford, in Cleveland Square, just off Bayswater. She was working part-time and I went to collect her one day from work. This was in the basement at Albion Street and I went down to ask if she was coming and the basement was full of people – there must have been 30 people in this grubby little basement at 1 Albion Street. They were all gaunt and looked like they'd never seen the sun for years.

"They were working like slaves putting this magazine together, rushing in and out with bundles of magazines and selling them on street corners. It was a hive of activity but it was somehow haunted; they were being chased as if the Devil was on their tails. I was impressed by this energy, even though it was a strange energy and they were all starving and they all had no money.

"So I played a bit of the knight in shining armour. I got in my van and drove off back to Queensway. There was a little mews behind Queensway that backed onto a Wimpy Bar and I drove my van down there. Outside this Wimpy Bar there were always polythene bags full of cups and uncooked chips waiting to be made into Wimpy chips. It was one of those things that you notice when you're fairly destitute – one notices hundredweight bags of chips and logs it away in the back of the mind for future reference! Anyway, this seemed the perfect thing so I went round and stole one of these great bags of chips and took it back to Albion Street. Everyone went bananas as if I was Jesus with the loaves and the fishes. They set upon these chips. All of a sudden frying pans appeared, gas cookers were lit and everybody took on a brighter aspect and everybody ate. There were chips, thousands of chips. For about three days everyone lived on chips!

"I had only ever seen the basement and I didn't instantly get to the bottom of what was motivating these people to do all this work for no money. Jackie was working there for two or three days, two or three evenings and a couple of afternoons a week. She was getting 15 bob, a reasonable amount of money then, but it was peanuts really, considering other people had proper jobs. During the course of the next month or two I got more and more curious about this phenomenon so I asked Jackie what it was all about, why they were all doing this.

"One rarely saw Richard; at least the people in the basement rarely saw Richard. There was a hierarchy in this house, which was completely taken over by Richard – it was some deal with the Church Commissioners that he had. There was a vicar at the end of the road – in fact we nearly built The Manor in his church!

"Anyway, eventually it struck me that if this guy's got this amount of power, maybe he's got a few bob and maybe there's room in this house for me to put some tape recorders and do my demos. I had a couple of old Ferrograph tape recorders and I was trying to get things together.

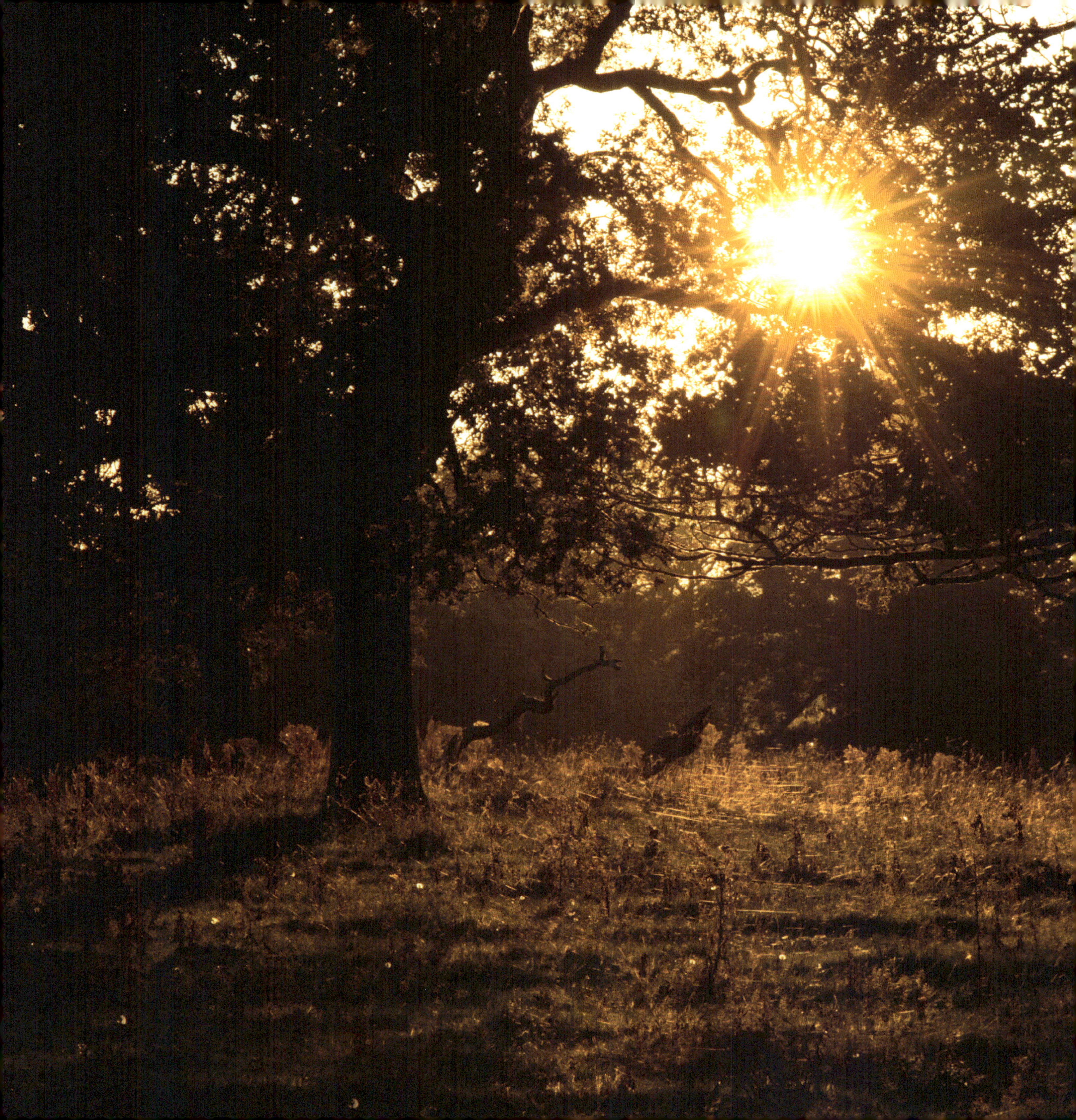

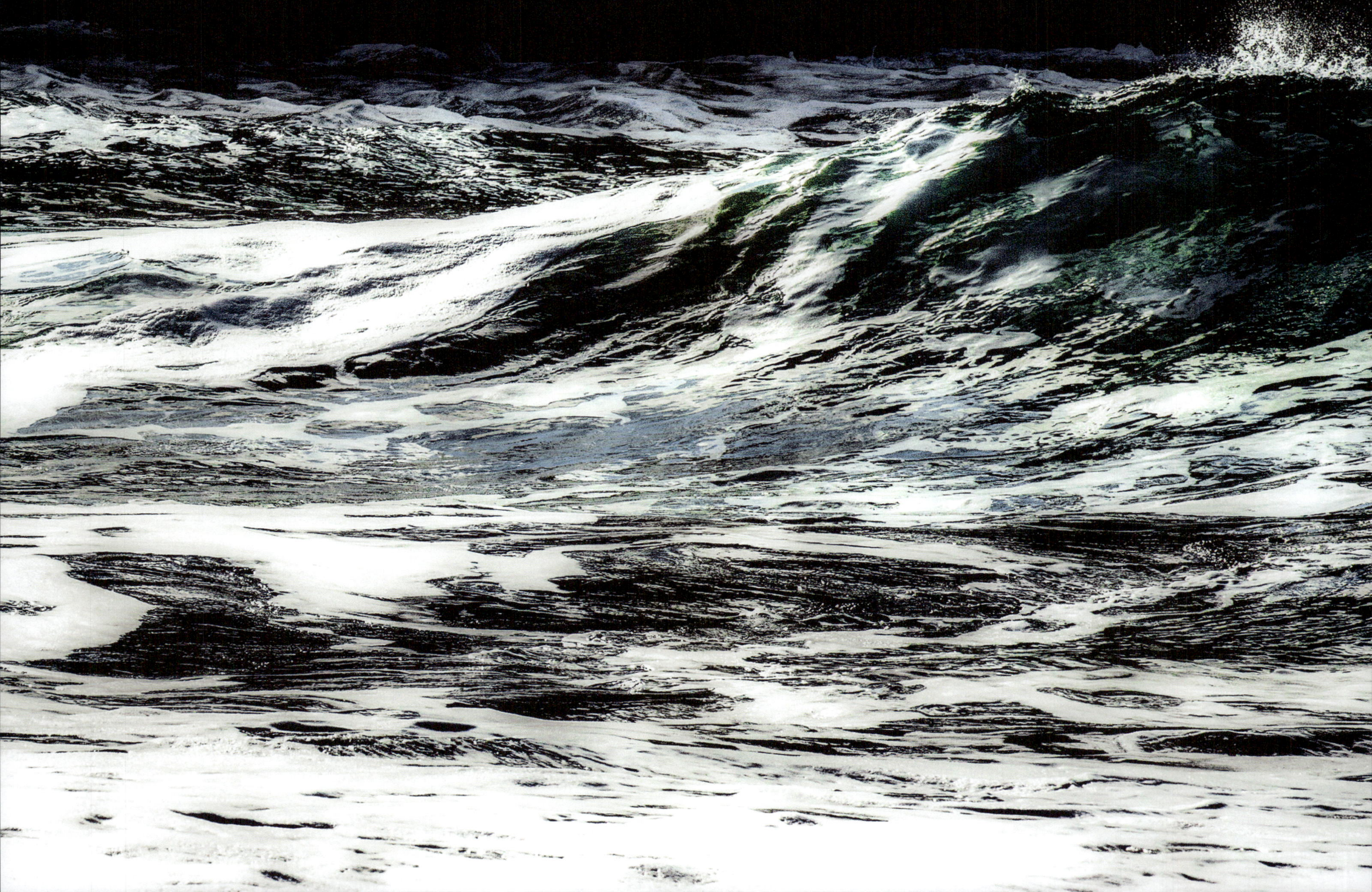

"So I just put it to him straight: 'Look, this would be a perfect set-up to have a recording studio and start a record label.'" TOM NEWMAN

"So I persuaded Jackie to introduce me to Richard with this as a pretext. I wanted to get a room in his house but I thought that was a bit cheeky, so maybe there would have to be something in it for him. I thought that maybe he would like to have a record company or something. I was just being a total opportunist; I had no idea what Richard was like or what was motivating him or anything about him. I just thought that this person and this situation had been put here for me to take advantage of. I was determined to somehow make something out of this.

"Eventually Jackie introduced me, took me upstairs, those winding stairs. It was all dead scruffy and on the very top floor, in the penthouse of this little Regency house, there was a 15ft square bedroom with a low ceiling and a big brass bed. There in the big brass bed, with a girl, was Richard; a young boy, a fresh-faced young lad with spectacles, who looked a bit like Alfred E. Neuman from 'Mad' magazine. A great, big mouth, big, gleaming teeth, constant smile, nice, steady gaze, and I liked him instantly. I liked him as soon as I clapped eyes on him and I had never met anybody like him before.

"He was younger than me by 10 years, but he was the first person I had ever met who was posh. I had never ever met a posh young man before because I was a working-class boy. I come from Wembley, I was born next to the Hoover factory and you were either from the council estate or you weren't.

"Richard had gone to Stowe, although I didn't know that at the time. So I was at once attracted by him because he was young and he was obviously powerful and I was curious because I couldn't believe that someone who was 10 years younger than me, which made him about 18, could control this whole houseful of working people, all working towards his dream.

"So I just put it to him straight: 'Look, this would be a perfect set-up to have a recording studio and start a record label.' He laughed and said he'd think about it. I didn't hear from him for a week or two and eventually Jackie said, 'Richard thinks it's a good idea: can you go and see him again?' So I went to see him and we sat down, talked about it and he asked if there was anywhere in the house. But the house was busy and not very secure.

"So we went to see The Reverend Cuthbert and he showed us the crypt of this church at the end of Albion Street. It was great; there were coffins and skeletons and all that stuff – and it was workable. It was arched, it was a vaulted ceiling, about eight feet high and quite extensive and it would have made a good studio. The vicar apparently agreed and started moving coffins about and trying to make a space, although I think he got a bit windy about the idea of moving the dead around. I did some plans about soundproofing and acoustic treatment – which I was making up as I went along, while reading copies of tape recorder magazines, desperately trying to keep one step ahead of what was happening."

"It really grasped my imagination, this whole idea of being inside this booth with the band outside; recording it remotely on this tape recorder and monitoring it ..." TOM NEWMAN

Tom Newman had already done some experimenting with recording musicians, using 'sound on sound'. Sound on sound is the technique which forms the basis for multitrack recording, whereby one musician can record different parts side by side and then play them back simultaneously.

Tom Newman: "That first happened during the course of being in a band. One automatically does recordings. In rehearsals with the July band, we used to record things in a bedroom, just for fun. The recorder was one of these ones that could do sound on sound; you could switch off the erase heads and get crude sound on sound. In fact, I recently found one or two tracks that we did in those days and it was surprisingly useable."

While in the blues-rock band, July, Tom Newman had his first experiences of being in a recording studio.

Tom Newman: "It really grasped my imagination, this whole idea of being inside this booth with the band outside; recording it remotely on this tape recorder and monitoring it, not being in the same room as the band and listening to it while it was going on. This was all intriguing stuff, albeit valve equipment and straight onto mono with three microphones. Great stuff! So I got the fire of wanting to know more about this recording business and to that end, while I was living with Jackie and during the early times of meeting Richard Branson, I took it upon myself to find out more.

"Through Exchange & Mart I bought two ex-Admiralty Vortexion tape recorders. They weren't bad, not exactly state-of-the-art, but they were close to it. You could bounce from one to the other and they had microphone amps and they had line output and they had proper VU meters. I did some demos on these tape records in Jackie Byford's flat and they were good. I experimented, doing as many bounces as I could, to see how many you could get between one machine and another.

"And I found, like Joe Meek and Phil Spector did, that the more bounces you did, the more atmosphere you could create. Even though the whole thing started to get fuzzy and not very clear round the edges, if you did it right and you were careful where you put the microphone and used a bit of echo, you could actually get some of the beginnings of what I started to translate as dynamics of sound. This idea became very important to me later on; the idea of sound not just being a one-dimensional thing being thrown at you, but there being sound in the foreground and sound in the background.

"This was something that was already well known to BBC sound effects engineers, of course. But I didn't go through all that school of learning so, to me, I was discovering. I was finding out that something that was echoey was actually further away from you and that was important. That suddenly gave colour to the whole thing and meant that I could have a sound that was distant yet loud. The sound of a loud guitar a long way away was very different from a loud guitar right in your ear. The poetry in that became very intriguing to me.

“The magical formula of colour, dimension, distance, space and size were the things that I found out in that year. There are still rules that if you don't understand will stop you getting any further. You need to know those things in order to do anything with sound … . TOM NEWMAN

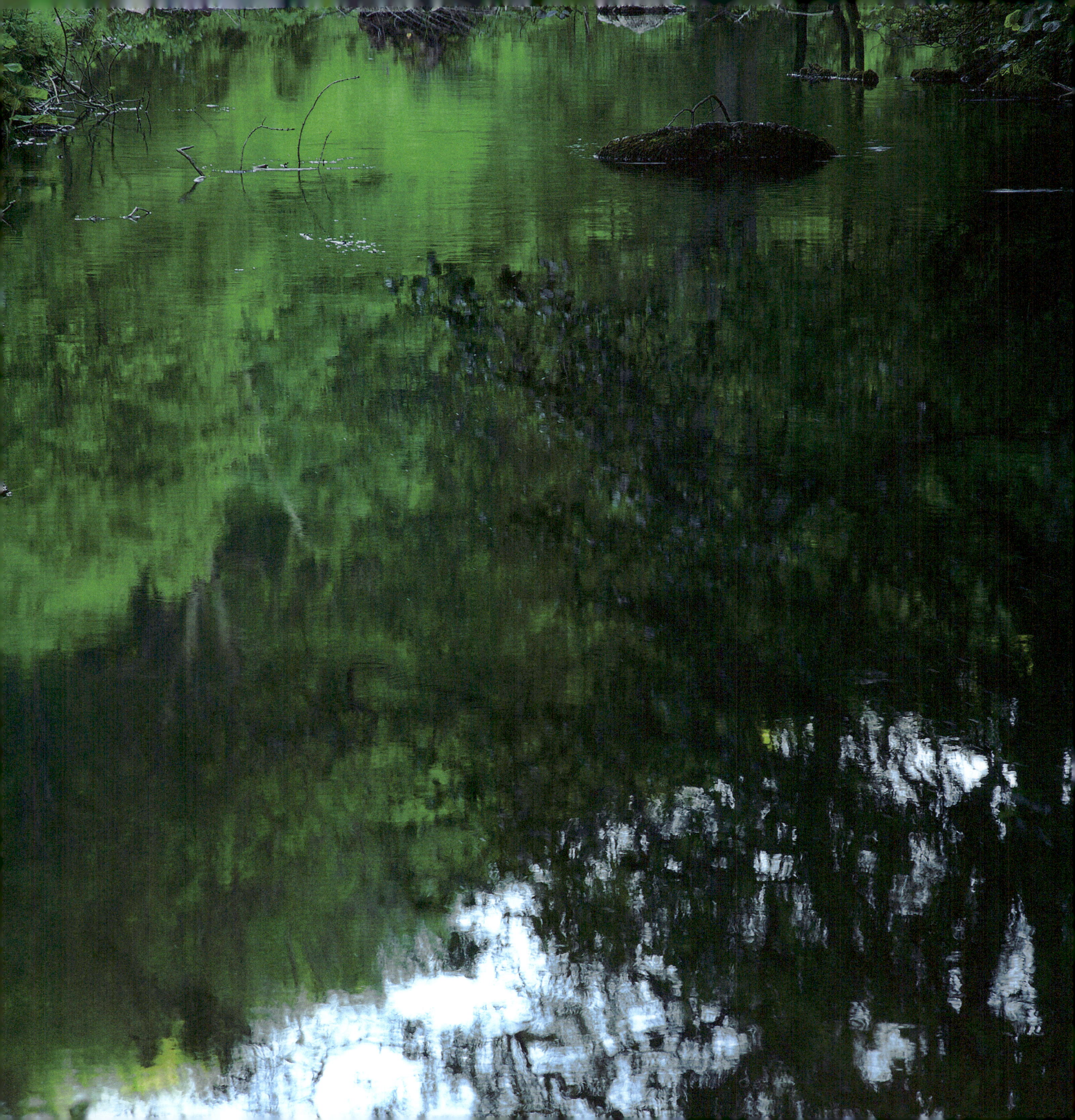

"The magical formula of colour, dimension, distance, space and size were the things that I found out in that year. There are still rules that if you don't understand will stop you getting any further. You need to know those things in order to do anything with sound and you can either find them out the hard way, like I did, or you can be taught them, if you are lucky enough to find yourself in that situation. Obviously now one can manipulate those things supremely well with the tools and the equipment that are available, virtually for nothing, but at that time it was a complete secret, a magician's art."

At exactly the same time as Tom Newman was finding out about sound recording, Mike Oldfield was also doing similar experiments with a tape recorder.

Tom Newman: "Yes, strangely enough, Michael was doing almost exactly the same thing at the same time. He had been doing little bits of demo on a Bang & Olufsen borrowed from Kevin Ayers. To get sound on sound he was putting a bit of sticky tape over the erase head. And so yes, we were doing very much the same thing."

Back at South Wharf Road Tom Newman continued to put pressure on Richard Branson with regard to the idea of a recording studio.

Tom Newman: "After we had gone to look at Cuthbert's Church I did some drawings and some plans about soundproofing and acoustic treatment. At that time George Martin, The Beatles' producer, lived in the same square as Cuthbert's Church, so Richard took my plans to him – I think partly to find out whether I knew what I was talking about – and George Martin came down and looked at the church. I met him and I was overwhelmed and very humble – he was an idol, he had done The Beatles – and fortunately he agreed with everything I had said, because it was just fairly logical. But he said it was really too small if we were serious, although it was all right for demos. But of course I was only looking at demos, I didn't care whether Richard made any money out of this, this was just for me, this was my studio and I was saying to myself: 'Shut up, George, never mind the decision, it's the demos I want. Blast you, go away!' I just wanted a space and if I could get some money out of Richard Branson to buy equipment so that I could do my demos, all well and good.

"I was very short-sighted and extremely selfish about this. I wasn't interested in the high-flown ideas of building a record company, really. That was just a dream that I was feeding Richard in order to get my evil way with him.

"What happened next was that Richard had given me a blank cheque to go out and buy a tape recorder and a mixer. So I had bought some equipment from a guy called Barry Gray, who wrote the Thunderbirds theme tune. He had a house in Kingston and he was moving – I think he went to Jamaica – so he was selling up his studio and I bought an Ampex 300 Series valve four-track, two Ampex monitor speaker amplifiers in portable cases, a couple of microphones, some mike stands, and a bunch of wiring.

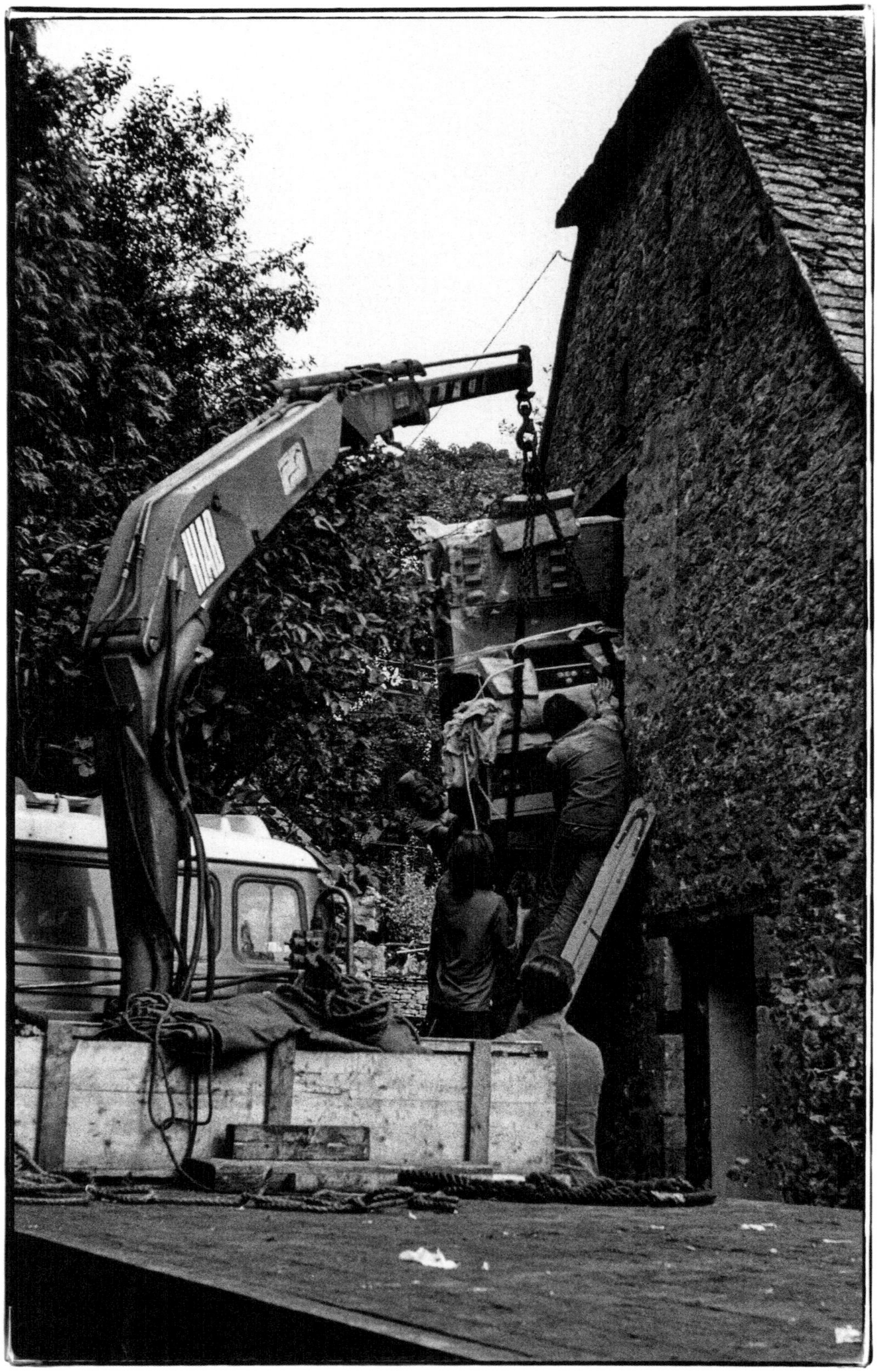

PHOTO: SIMON HEYWORTH

Craning the 16-track tape machine into the control room

"… whilst musing and daydreaming, waiting to see Richard, I thought, 'Wouldn't it be great if we could have a studio in a place like that?'" TOM NEWMAN

"As well as thinking the church too small, George Martin had just gone eight-track and so told us we ought to be thinking eight-track rather than four-track. Richard obviously then thought that at least I knew what I was talking about, even if I was a little bit behind. So he started to trust me.

"The relationship was fine. I think he was fascinated by my sense of initiative. He found it interesting because he had it as well, but in a different way. Richard had initiative when it came to manipulating people. He had the ability to get people to do things for him, whereas I wouldn't have been able to do that, because I wouldn't have had the gall to confront 20 people with a task that I wouldn't do, so why should I ask other people to do it? I came from this working-class background of not wanting to ask anyone else to do something that I couldn't do myself.

"So a certain amount of trust was growing up between us in our respective fields and I became more and more convinced that Richard would be able to supply the wherewithal for me to do my demos. Obviously that was not something I told him! So I would go along with anything that Richard wanted to do because I was convinced that this was an interval in my life that was a positive one.

"I was then introduced to someone else who became important in the Virgin hierarchy later on, a guy called Phil Newell who was a recording engineer at Pye Studios. I met him because the next step in the game was to go eight-track. Richard said, 'Look, this four-track is all very well, but everyone has gone eight-track and we ought to catch up.' So I started buying 'Studio Sound' and seeing what I could do with eight-track. I went to a place called Majestic, which was selling some eight-track mixing equipment and there I met Phil Newell, who was working part-time there and also part-time at Pye Records.

"At the time he sold me on this enormous eight-track console. He had built it from the neck up and it was valve and I wish I had kept it; I mean, now it would be worth hundreds of thousands of pounds but I think we paid about three or four hundred quid for it. It was gigantic and it had millions of quids' worth of transformers in it, and valves and everything. It was beautifully made. It had been up and working once, but then it had had teething troubles and Phil was in the middle of sorting these out. The guy who owned the studio wasn't prepared to spend the time and wanted something that was instantly going to work, so they had to sell it. Anyway, Richard signed the cheque, we bought it and it was stored in the other house at Albion Street for a time, because we had nowhere to put it.

"Meanwhile we still had the four-track and so it was becoming crucial to find somewhere to put all of this equipment. I was looking at a Country Life magazine one day in Albion Street while waiting to see Richard. I spotted this house in Oxfordshire in its own grounds; it just looked beautiful and it was 30 thousand quid, which might as well have been 20 million! But whilst musing and daydreaming, waiting to see Richard, I thought, 'Wouldn't it be great if we could have a studio in a place like that?'

“Richard and I loved The Manor and we thought, ‘Let’s do the studio in the squash court.’ ” TOM NEWMAN

“It had a squash court, and I didn’t know what a squash court was; I didn’t even know whether that was inside or outside. Anyway, I took the magazine up with me when I went to see Richard and I said, ‘Look at that, what a house, what about a studio in a house like that?’ Nothing! It didn’t really go in, but maybe it did. Anyway, I pursued it half-heartedly every now and then at every opportunity. I mentioned that we needed somewhere for the studio, that we’ve got this enormous console sitting around doing nothing and we need to find premises.”

In due course Branson was convinced and so he and Tom Newman went on an expedition to see the house.

Tom Newman: “Without an appointment, we climbed over the wall and looked around. The second time we went we made an appointment and we met Mr Branch, the gardener, who showed us around. The first ghost story came out of that …

“We had taken Richard’s secretary, a girl called Caroline, and she was wandering about at one end of The Manor while we were wandering around the grounds. She was upstairs in the servants’ quarters, as they were then, and she met this lady who she assumed was with Mr Branch. She was talking to her and they had a five-minute conversation about the house and presently we all met up and went back to town. Nothing more was said. It didn’t actually have any significance until we had bought The Manor and moved in. It was the Christmas of ’71. We had a house-warming party and during the course of the party Caroline was wandering around, as one does, and we were going through the attics.

“We found this pile of old artefacts and they began to accumulate on a table in the hallway. Amongst these was a photograph, an old sepia print, half worn out. It was of a lady standing next to a 1940s Ford V8 Pilot station wagon, holding a dead pike. She was obviously a sportswoman. She was in tweeds and Caroline said, ‘Oh look, there’s the lady I met when we first came down; that’s the lady who I was talking to.’ Again, we thought nothing more of it.

“Then, during the period of actually moving in, which was early spring 1971, the picture was lying on the table. One day I mentioned to Mr Branch that we hadn’t seen this lady again and that she had been around when we first came. I assumed that it might have been a relative. He said, ‘Oh, that was one of the previous owners, she died 15 years ago.’ And the hair stood up on the back of my neck! I told Caroline and she went as white as a sheet!

“Richard and I loved The Manor and we thought, ‘Let’s do the studio in the squash court.’ There was a barn next door with the squash court in it and this was perfect for a studio.

“It was a little stable with a hayloft above, which I converted into the control room. I immediately started drawing pictures and designing it, while Richard went off to try and find the money. I was perfectly convinced that he would find the money, although to me £30,000 was impossible. He went to his Aunty Joyce and Aunty Joyce came up with the money and I thought, ‘Well, born with a silver spoon, hoi polloi.’

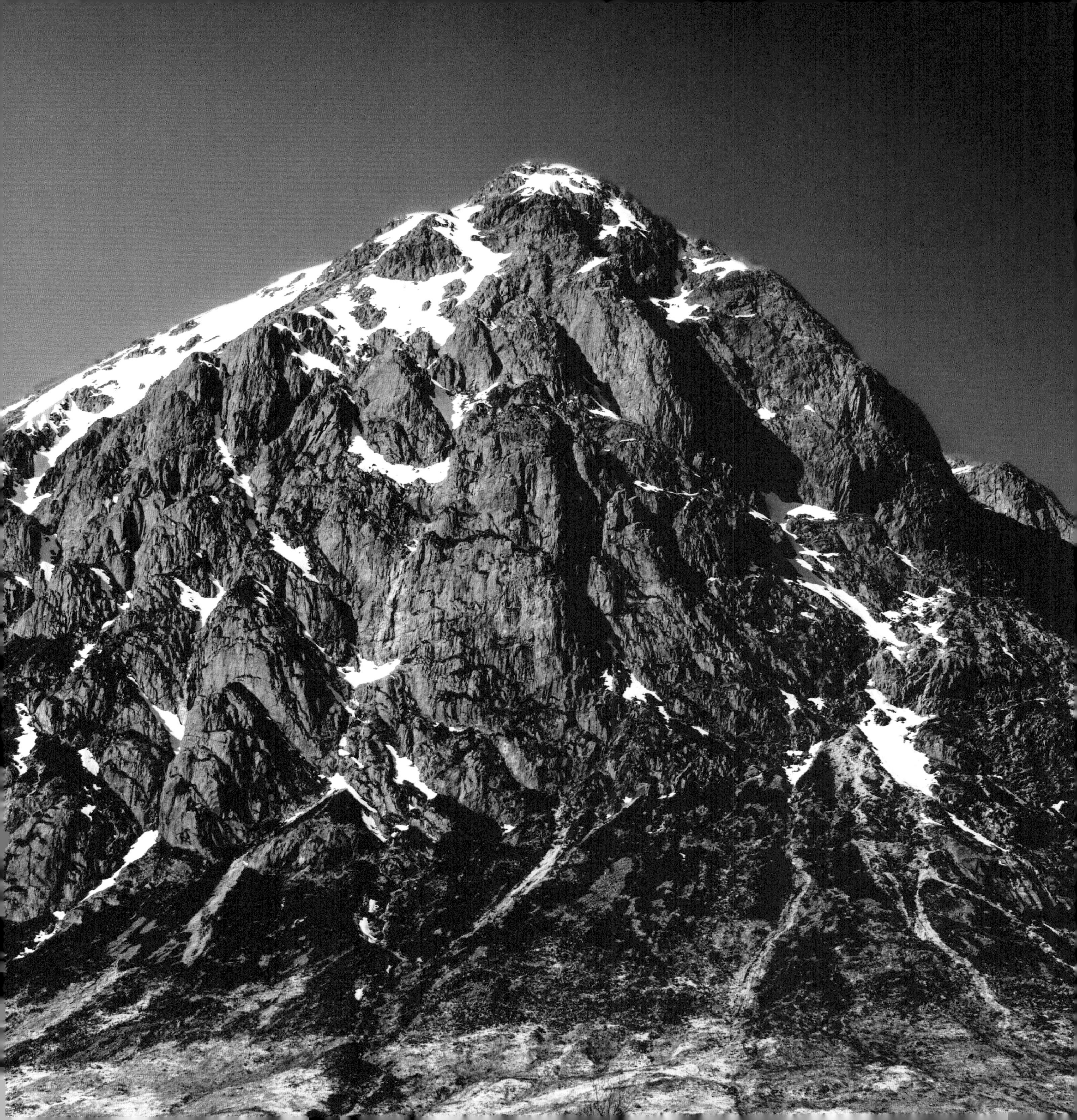

“

It was a really lovely little tune that was meandering and plaintive and it made my heart burst. It was beautiful and I just wanted to be part of it. I can’t explain what I mean, but it was so beautiful. It was like a Pied Piper of Hamelin situation … . TOM NEWMAN

"In fact it was a terrible deal. His Aunty Joyce didn't do him any favours at all; it was a straightforward mortgage and he had to pay it every month.

"We kept South Wharf Road as the offices and we moved into The Manor and I started moving equipment in. I picked a team of guys to help me, amongst whom was Phil Newell who was helping in the first stages, and I met a guy called Johnnie Barwick who came down. He was a big, stroppy guy, a Newcastle lad, a long-haired hippy. He became the head of the labouring team. A guy called Alan Joyce was also on the labouring team.

"I went to London one day and I was in the office and this lad came in and introduced himself. I can't remember where he came from, or why he was there, but his name was Simon Heyworth. He was such a nice guy that I took him on straight away and said, 'Come on down to The Manor now.' So we got in the car and off we went. It was instant chemistry; I got on with Simon straight away, he was such a nice bloke, I had no reservations about him whatsoever. He said, 'I'll do anything.'

"The first I said was, 'Are you an engineer? What can you do?' And he said, 'I dunno, I'll do anything you like,' with his great, big, horsey grin. So what could I say? We started work and began tearing bits of walls down and building walls up and generally doing what was needed.

"I supposed we had been there a little while, a week or two working away, and 'Sticky Fingers' by The Rolling Stones came out. Simon got the record and we set up the sounds in the studio where we were working. We had this enormous great echoey squash court and I'd bought a pair of BBC loudspeakers and a pair of old Quad valve amps. So we set the sounds up and worked away to 'Sticky Fingers' all day long, singing and learning. We played it to death, right through one side and out the other; it was a constant thing all day long.

"We had a local builder in to do the structural alterations because there was work that had to be done professionally. Bill Palmer, who was a lovely old bloke, was the head of the building team. We became Bill's navvies after a while – for the first bits anyway – and then there was the electronics team which was really Phil Newell and a guy called Dave Hughes.

"We started off and it was going to be an eight-track. While the actual studio building was being built there was pressure to get something happening soundwise. One of the rooms in the downstairs of the house, which was originally the library, was converted into a control room and the next room into a studio. So I set up this enormous valve eight-track mixer that we had got from Phil Newell in one of the downstairs rooms.

"Phil used to come down at the weekends and do wiring and generally get the thing working. Eventually we got it up and running, along with the four-track Ampex and a couple of stereo machines and bits and pieces. So we had a rudimentary studio that was just about useable, but there were still teething troubles and still a lot of things we didn't have.

"You have this bunch of slightly itinerant, dreamer-type people who suddenly find themselves in this beautiful country house in the middle of Oxfordshire." TOM NEWMAN

"I was very tenuously commander-in-chief. Phil knew a lot more about it than I did, technically speaking, so I didn't really know what I was talking about. I was learning from Phil but still the boss of the whole operation. You learn quickly under those circumstances!

"Eventually we got it all working and the first thing that happened was that this band arrived – we got about one day's notice that there was a band coming down to try out the studio!"

The band was The Arthur Lewis Band and the guitar player was Mike Oldfield.

Tom Newman: "It was a completely abysmal session because things were breaking down and things didn't work as one would expect. We were also on the cusp of deciding whether to now go sixteen-track or not, but the financial problem was there. Sixteen-track was the state-of-the-art at the time and that meant buying new, rather than second-hand, so it was a very big step. I was in the middle of making an eight-track machine, the mechanical side of it, and I got Phil to agree to build the modules. I bought an old computer deck that I was converting to work as a tape recorder.

"So this band arrived at a day or two's notice but we did a creditable job and things got put onto tape, albeit only in four-track. They were demos and at least we found out the limitations of the system and there was a buzz because we had actually recorded something. That strengthened the resolve to finish building the studio.

"Richard wanted to apply pressure. He saw the building as something that was going to drag on, so it was a wise move really. Life at The Manor was a very easy situation to just exist in. You have this bunch of slightly itinerant, dreamer-type people who suddenly find themselves in this beautiful country house in the middle of Oxfordshire. And there was no money – we were getting 12 quid a week!

"One of the girls brought the money over on Sunday or Monday, or sometime over the weekend. The trouble was it wasn't regular; sometimes we didn't have it and sometimes we would miss a week. There were constant phone calls: me shouting at Richard Branson, 'We haven't got any money; send some money down; Bill Palmer wants paying; this wants paying.' Constant demands.

"Richard would say, 'Well, all right, all right, all right, but when are we going to be up and running?' It must have been a nightmare from his point of view. He would come down every other weekend and see the progress and it seemed to him, I'm sure, that there was a constant set of problems.

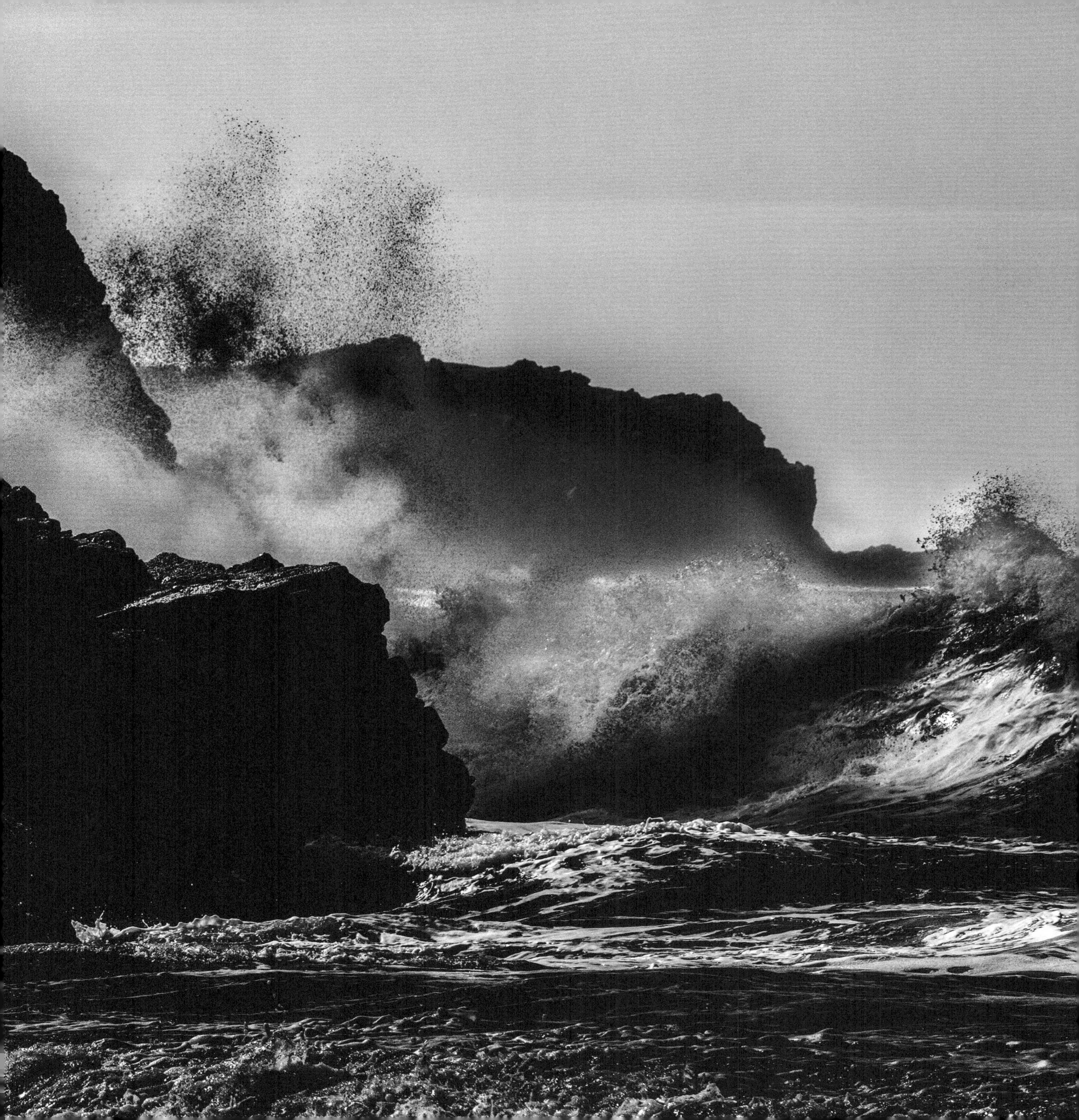

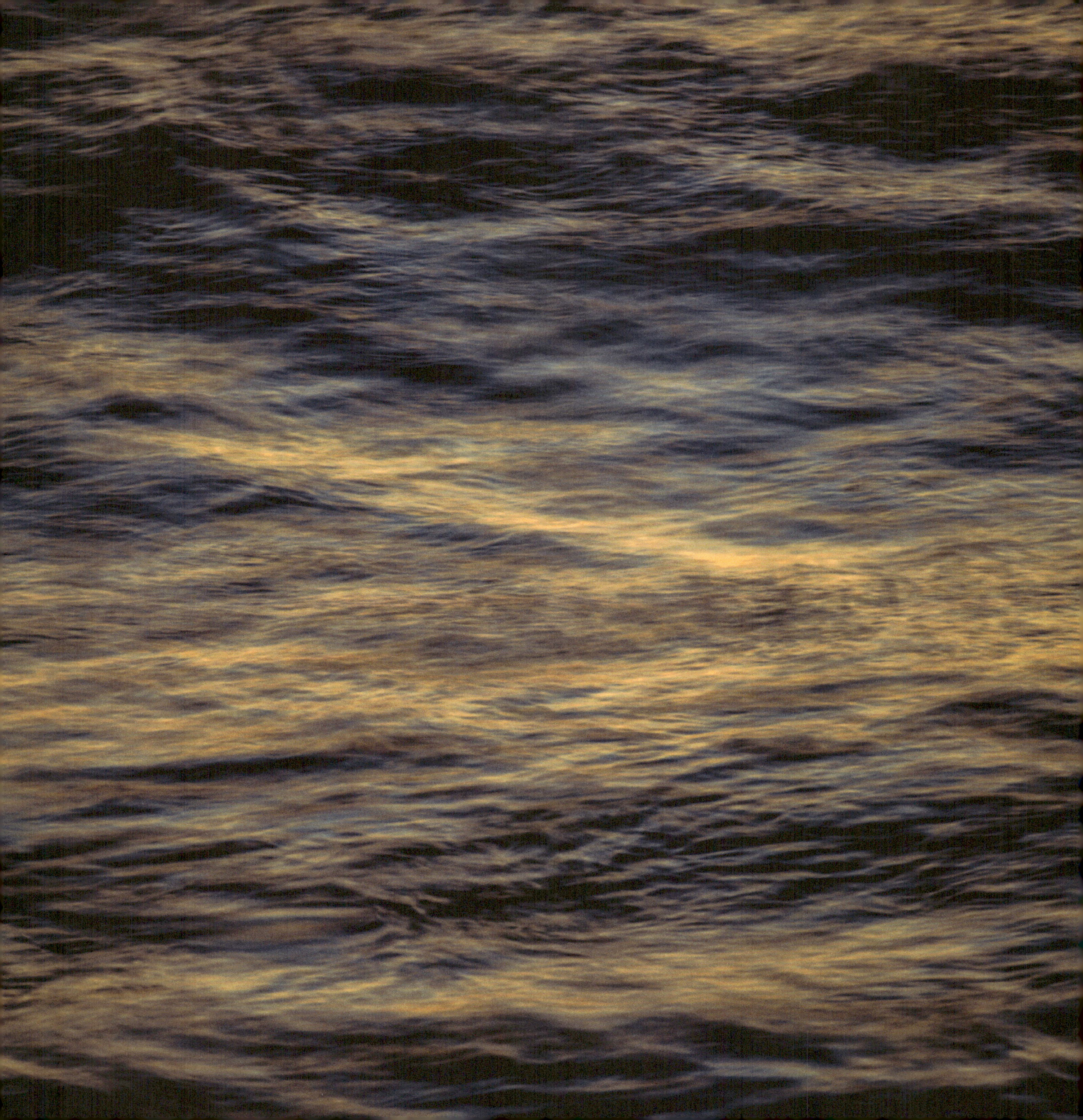

"It was like a Pied Piper of Hamelin situation: if Michael had gone off with this tape and said, 'Follow me', I'd have followed him to the ends of the earth." TOM NEWMAN

"And there was. There were always problems. It wasn't easy to build a studio from nothing, when you had never built a studio before. And because we were making it up as we went along, we were trying to keep that from Richard – we didn't want Richard to think that we were too incompetent at what we were doing. We were also having a good time and the original idea of me doing demos was getting muzzy around the edges. It was being overtaken by the whole idea of this being a wonderful place. I was thinking, 'How can I keep this going?' Richard's enthusiasm for a record label and Richard's whole attitude to life, the way he looked at life, was impressing me and I was changing.

"I suddenly saw a different thing. I had never heard anything as good as the demos that Michael played me. It was exactly like those icebergs that stick up, like 'Albatross', like 'Ghost Riders', like 'Love is Strange', like 'Kites'.

"After I had heard the music, I suddenly felt there was a kindred soul there somewhere. So I took him down the pub and got him drunk on Guinness, because we both drank draught Guinness by the gallon. I had a pal called Mick Taylor – not The Stones' guitar player – who was at The Manor as well. He was one of the other people who were involved in the early days, purely on a building basis, and he was there for a year or so. He was like Simon Heyworth, a great supporter of the project; he was a drinking partner and we used to take Mike Oldfield down the pub and get him drunk!

"We would get him to play and he would play at the most inopportune or strangest of moments. He would pick up and play the most beautiful stuff on anything that was lying around. It could be an old scruffy mandolin or whatever, but he just played. It was gorgeous stuff, the likes of which I had never heard. He wasn't into keyboards at the time, he was a guitarist.

"One part of the demo that got me, and I don't know why, is the one I remember that never got on 'Tubular Bells'. There was a little theme that Michael did that had, as a backing track, a domestic Hoover. He had a Hoover at his house in Harold Hill and he did this thing with it and it played this strange suspended minor seventh chord; a really lovely sound, like a drone. It was this Hoover making the sound, and it was like a bagpipe drone.

"It was a really lovely little tune that was meandering and plaintive and it made my heart burst. It was beautiful and I just wanted to be part of it. I can't explain what I mean, but it was so beautiful. It was like a Pied Piper of Hamelin situation: if Michael had gone off with this tape and said, 'Follow me', I'd have followed him to the ends of the earth. I'd never heard anything like it before in my life."

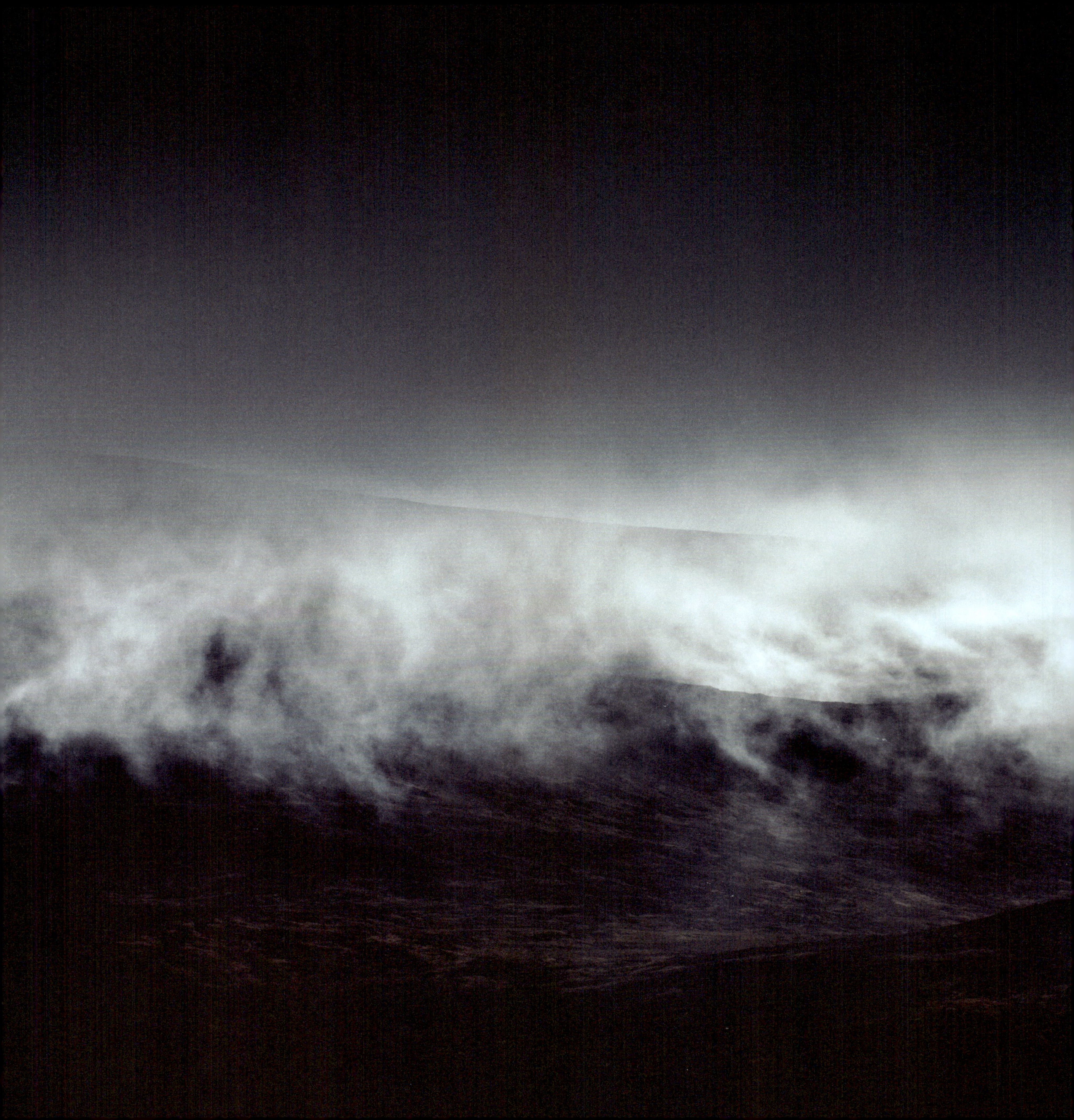

3

THE RECORDING OF 'TUBULAR BELLS'

*M**IKE OLDFIELD** was now living at The Manor permanently and in the spirit of the communal atmosphere he offered to help Tom Newman with the actual building work.*

Tom Newman: "He was useless, but we both liked model aeroplanes so we built the odd model while he was there. We were still building the studio, but by this time we had gone sixteen-track and we had ordered a mixer. It was a professional mixer that was being built for us by Audio Developments up in Staffordshire, and whilst waiting for that to arrive we were finishing building the rest of the studio."

Eventually the first 'official' recording session took place. This was for the Bonzo Dog Band.

Tom Newman: "We didn't start work until February '73 when the Bonzo Dog Band came in. That was the next 'hurry up' thing that Richard Branson dropped on us, because again he could see us slowing down so he booked a band in.

"We were still wiring the studio when they arrived. They were only meant to be there a week to do an album, but they ended up being there for getting on for two months because of teething troubles with the studio. Things weren't right but it was great, we had great fun. Again, we couldn't have had a better first band because they got into the feel of the community.

PHOTO: SIMON HEYWORTH

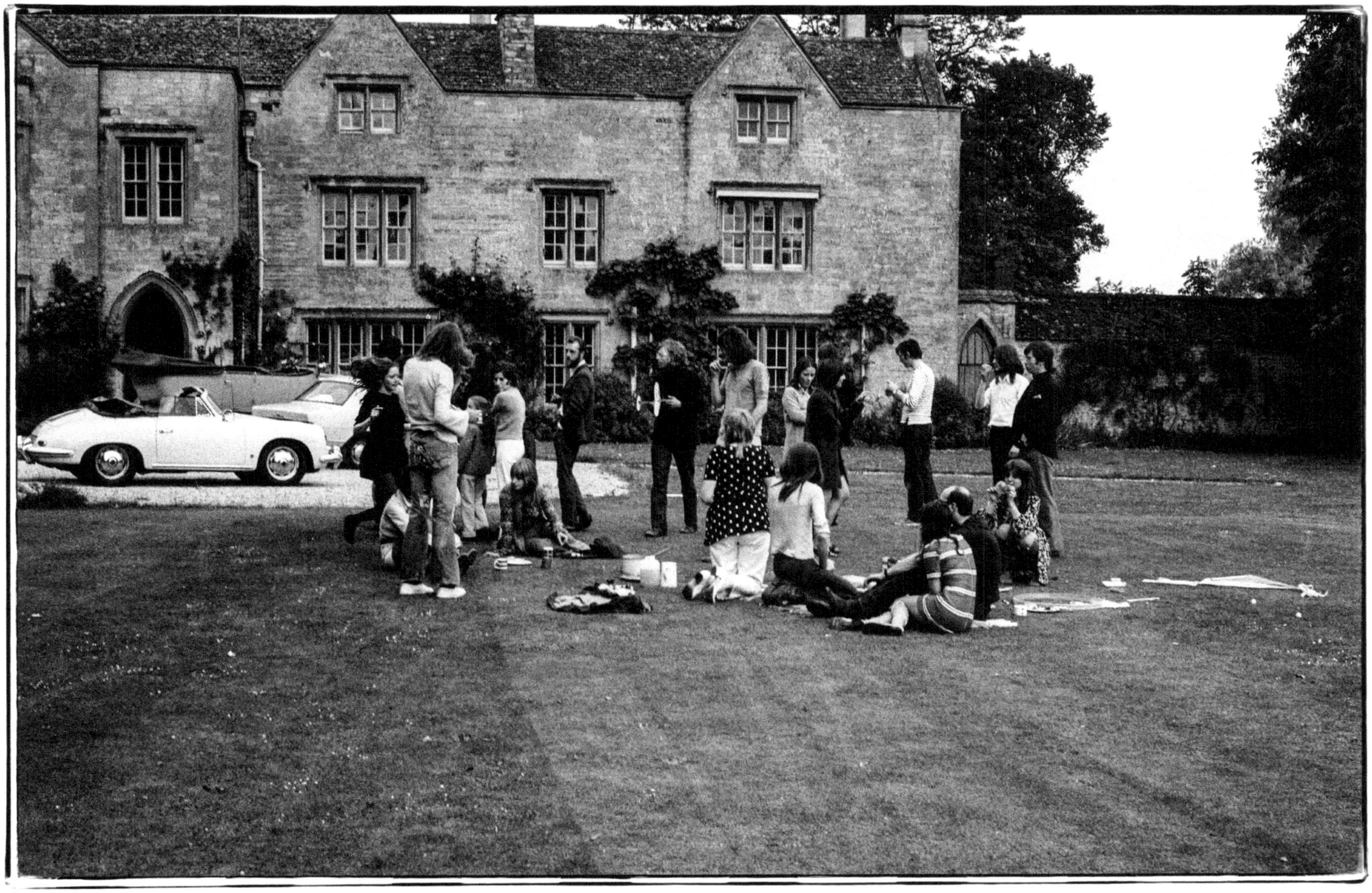

A party at The Manor: Branson (centre) holds a toy aeroplane, perhaps already planning his future strategy

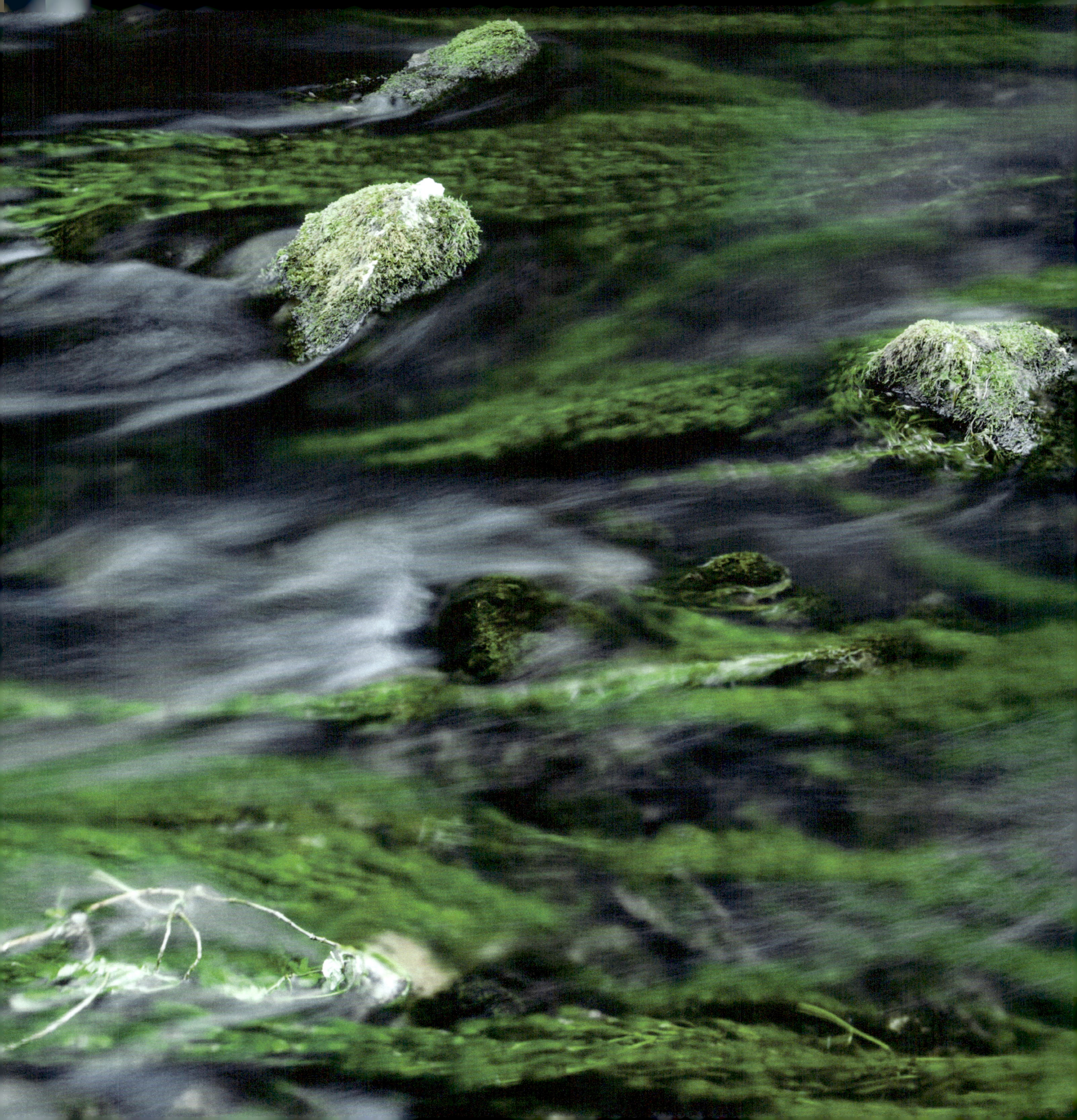

"Michael was there all the time ... we got very close. It got so brotherly that we used to wrestle on the lawn, but I cracked one of his ribs wrestling one day." TOM NEWMAN

"They were hippies as well, or at least they were intellectuals. They weren't raving popstars and they felt the same verve and commune that we all felt.

"Michael was there all the time and we were building these model aeroplanes. We got very close. It got so brotherly that we used to wrestle on the lawn, but I cracked one of his ribs wrestling one day.

"Michael helped with the Bonzos now and then because it was an ongoing thing. I was trying to teach him, because I really needed all the help I could get.

"On the very first Bonzo sessions I sat down as the engineer and Phil Newell was the tape operator. Phil knew how to do it and I didn't, but I had to do the session because I was supposed to be the main man there, otherwise what was I there for? However, I didn't know how to do it. I didn't know how to mike up a drum kit; I just put mikes there and hoped it would work.

"I was talking to Phil Newell all the time while he was sitting at the tape recorder. Of course, this was before you had remote control so you had to have a tape op sitting at the tape machine and you would shout 'Track 13 and record. On my mark, three, two, one – in'. That was how you did it.

"So, in all truth, the engineer was the tape op and I was acting out the engineer's role, except that I didn't know what to do. Anytime I didn't know what to do next I would go over to Phil and say, 'What do I do now?' I'd make the pretence of saying, 'Oh Phil, let's get it together', and all the time I was really saying, 'What the fuck do I do? How do I do this? How do I do that? And what do they mean, 'foldback'?

"Mike Oldfield was around all of the time then, whenever there was spare studio time in between the Bonzo sessions – as there was, since occasionally they had other commitments and they'd leave for a few days. Another factor was that the Bonzos were a big band and some of them would be asleep while some of them would work. Because of that we found ourselves doing 18- or 20-hour days, so Simon Heyworth would take over from me and then Mike Oldfield would take over from Simon. We were engineering one week and tape opping the next.

"But we were all referring to Phil Newell because he was the only one who knew anything technically, so I suppose you could say Phil was there as the grand-daddy. We constantly referred to him when we were in trouble and that way we were able to keep the whole thing going. It was Phil who maintained it and he lined up all the machines etc., but myself and Simon, and to a certain extent Mick Taylor and Michael, were very much involved. We were all working away learning, and this osmosis was happening where we were feeding off each other and taking the sessions and managing to keep it all together.

"I occasionally talked to Richard Branson and obviously saw him at the weekends every now and then. He would start food fights, he would come down and be the gay young squire doing his thing. He would entertain the bands by acting the fool.

"Michael was very quiet at that time. He was excited but I could tell he was excited because he was so quiet." TOM NEWMAN

"I was the only personality down there who was upfront enough to carry the day-to-day running of the place. Then John Aden came as an accountant, because I was useless at figures and Simon Heyworth hated figures, so none of us wanted to do any proper paperwork. It ended up as myself and Simon running the show with Phil Newell in the background."

At this point Richard Branson and his second in command at Virgin, Simon Draper, had not actually committed themselves to taking on 'Tubular Bells'. Eventually, however, the beseeching to Draper and Branson paid off.

Tom Newman: "I think Michael had also kept on at them and it got to a point where I went to London, talked seriously about doing 'Tubular Bells' with Simon Draper, Nik Powell (then organising the financial affairs at Virgin) and Richard Branson. Michael wasn't there at the time. Simon Draper phoned Michael, then Michael and I sat down at The Manor and talked about the structure and how he wanted to do it and then we started.

"I can only suppose that Simon Draper was as affected by it as I was. During the time between starting the studio proper and the beginning of the recording, I prompted and phoned and pestered Simon Draper and Richard Branson maybe half a dozen times. Because every time Michael appeared he said, 'Have you spoken to Richard recently?' He constantly barracked me, so I said, 'No, I'll phone him.' So I would phone Richard, or whoever I could get."

Tom Newman insists that, although Oldfield had some ideas which he wanted to include in 'Tubular Bells', they were by no means formulated into an organised structure.

Tom Newman: "Michael had some basic ideas. He had the riff at the front of side one and the Caveman idea (listed on the album as Piltdown Man). He had other bits of melody but they weren't properly connected and he wasn't sure which bits would follow which. He knew what would come first and he knew the first couple of changes, but he got lost around the part when the acoustic guitar came in. It was loosely together, but nothing was rigidly fixed.

"But Michael had this fire in his belly. He hustled me because I was the only person he could hustle. He found me in someone who was as close as he could ever get to and so he had no inhibitions about hustling me.

"Michael was very quiet at that time. He was excited but I could tell he was excited because he was so quiet. He was a quiet person anyway, but there was quiet and there were qualities of quietness that you could divine in him if you knew him.

"When we went in Michael had done another demo, but this one didn't mean much to me. For some reason I didn't like it that much, partly because the bits that I'd really loved from the original tape were not there. For instance, I was really pissed off that the Hoover tune wasn't there, but he wouldn't hear of it.

PHOTO: SIMON HEYWORTH

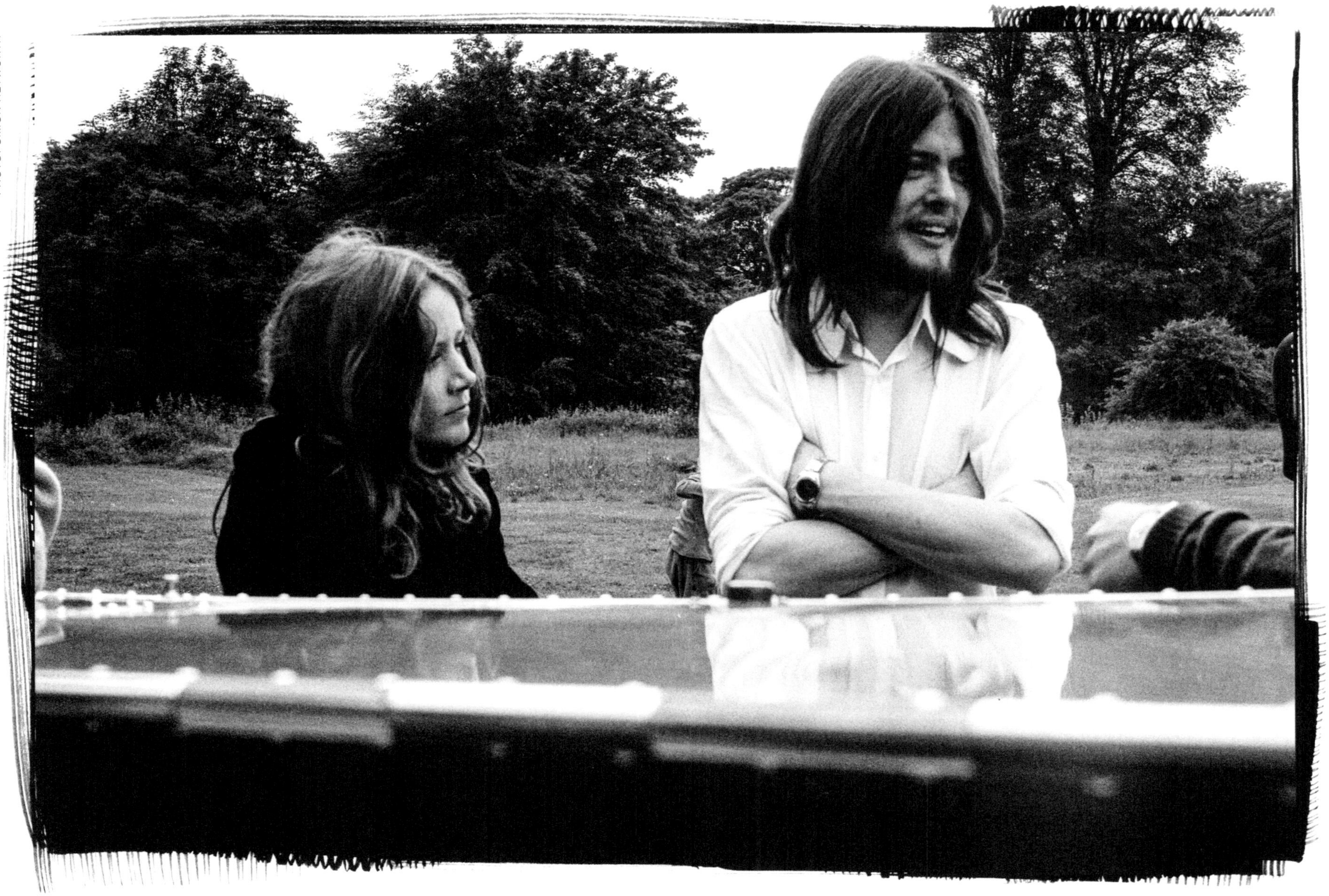

Jackie Byford and Tom Newman

"It was relatively new format, certainly compared to the way that it is today. It was in its infant years." SIMON HEYWORTH

"But we got on with it. We went in, miked up the piano and tried to get down the first riff. But we found it was really difficult because he couldn't play in time. I'd never been that worried about tempo anyway, but it was not good enough even for me. So we tried for the first day or two to get his timing right and wasted a lot of hours working out a method of doing it. I tried a tape loop, made a loop of the first little instrumental section, the opening motif, but I couldn't get it to feel right. I couldn't get one that felt like it wasn't a tape loop!

"Eventually we tried it with a metronome and that worked out well. We put the glockenspiel down – de dink de dink dink dink – all the way through. We put a lot of that on until it seemed like long enough. Then we put the piano part on top of that, and then he played bass on that. We built it up like that and just kept it going until it felt like it ought to change. Then we would drop something else in on top of that and rub the rest of the track out at the point when we felt it ought to change. Then we started on the next bit, dropping in at that point.

"Michael seemed to know what sections he wanted to come next, but he wasn't fully clear about how to get from one bit to another, technically – whether it should be a clean, straight thing or whether it should fade out of one thing and into another. We tried all sorts of things and eventually ended up with what we ended up with. Simon Heyworth was tape op at that point.

"The week progressed and Michael worked intensively. Simon and I tended to swap over sometimes. Simon would get up early if I had done a late session and vice versa. We worked from about 10 or 11 o'clock in the morning through until 2 o'clock the next morning. So it was a 14- or 15-hour day, with a break in the middle and sometimes a break to go out and adjust the head.

"But none of us started off knowing anything about multitrack recording."

Simon Heyworth agrees.

Simon Heyworth: "It was relatively new format, certainly compared to the way that it is today. It was in its infant years."

Tom Newman: "It was developed in order to get a 'Sgt. Pepper ...' sound, because of the fact that 'Sgt. Pepper ...' had introduced multitrack recording in a way that we now know it, even though they'd achieved it in a very different way. They had used two four-track machines and bounced between them, but the sixteen-track was meant to be used in a situation where you put the backing tracks down on four tracks and then used a stereo pair to put backing vocals on, a stereo pair to put string sections on, a stereo pair to put percussion on etc. That was the way it seemed to be working in the London studios. They used it as a way of building up something that would normally have been a complete performance recorded with two microphones straight onto a stereo machine, or a three-track machine or a four-track machine with bits added to it, like the vocals. But the thing about 'Tubular Bells' was that we started to use it in a different way."

Simon Heyworth: "A completely different way. In those days everything was balanced as acoustic instruments. So you recorded your four tracks or six tracks of drum kit and bass guitar and so on, then you added these extra tracks and the whole thing was easy to mix. It was a real cinch, and that was it.

"When we came to do 'Tubular Bells' it was a question of starting right from the beginning. Mike had done an interesting thing with his tape machine: it was a quarter-track machine with two tracks going one way and two tracks going the other way. What he'd done was to cover the erase head over, with a bit of cardboard, so you got four tracks going in one direction. That was clever. But when we finally started recording it onto sixteen-track, it was literally a question of doing it one track at a time, which was a completely different concept. And not only that, the instruments went on for ages!"

Tom Newman: "There was a piano part on side one that went on for 15 minutes in one go. And then we added things to that. That meant getting the playing in time, because Michael wasn't a technically good keyboard player then and we had to muck about with putting a metronome on and then feeding it to him in the headphones – these are standard ways of using multitrack equipment now, but at that time one person playing everything presented certain problems."

Simon Heyworth: "What tended to happen was you'd get the first couple of minutes as a really nice performance, but then it would start to slip out of time. So you'd stop it and then you'd get bollocked for stopping it because it was a good performance. The point was that if you'd built up three or four tracks of that, and then it all went out of time; the whole thing was going to sound a mess. We got into those situations quite regularly where we'd be floundering around saying, 'But something's sending the whole thing out of time.' Then of course the time spent doing that was very intense; you'd forget where you were and start rubbing things out that were already on the track! It became a real nightmare in terms of the concept of multitrack recording. It was very, very difficult at times."

Tom Newman: "I think we got the whole piano part down in one go, after many tries and fiddling and trying to drop in. I mean, dropping in was impossible because the technology of the tape recorder was such that you could drop in, but there was a big gap if you tried to drop out. Of course, things like that have been long cured, but back then dropping in was fraught with problems. Even the drop-in itself, you had to get it on some musical beat because there was always a little thump or something; it wasn't actually clean, even with a two-inch, so-called 'professional' machine. So we ended up, eventually, doing the whole thing in one go, but it took a fair while to get it to that stage."

Simon Heyworth: "It was our learning curve, really. And there was a learning curve for Mike Oldfield in many respects, because he began to understand the process and he began to understand how a piece of music would sound. I think a lot of the frustrations that occurred on both sides were part of that learning process. Then suddenly you'd get a performance back. That was always the thing that we were after.

“

It was a very magical time, especially the way that the sessions just organically rolled on. What made it organic was that none of us had an absolutely dyed-in-the-wool attitude or idea about what the future held. Whatever happened tomorrow happened tomorrow. TOM NEWMAN

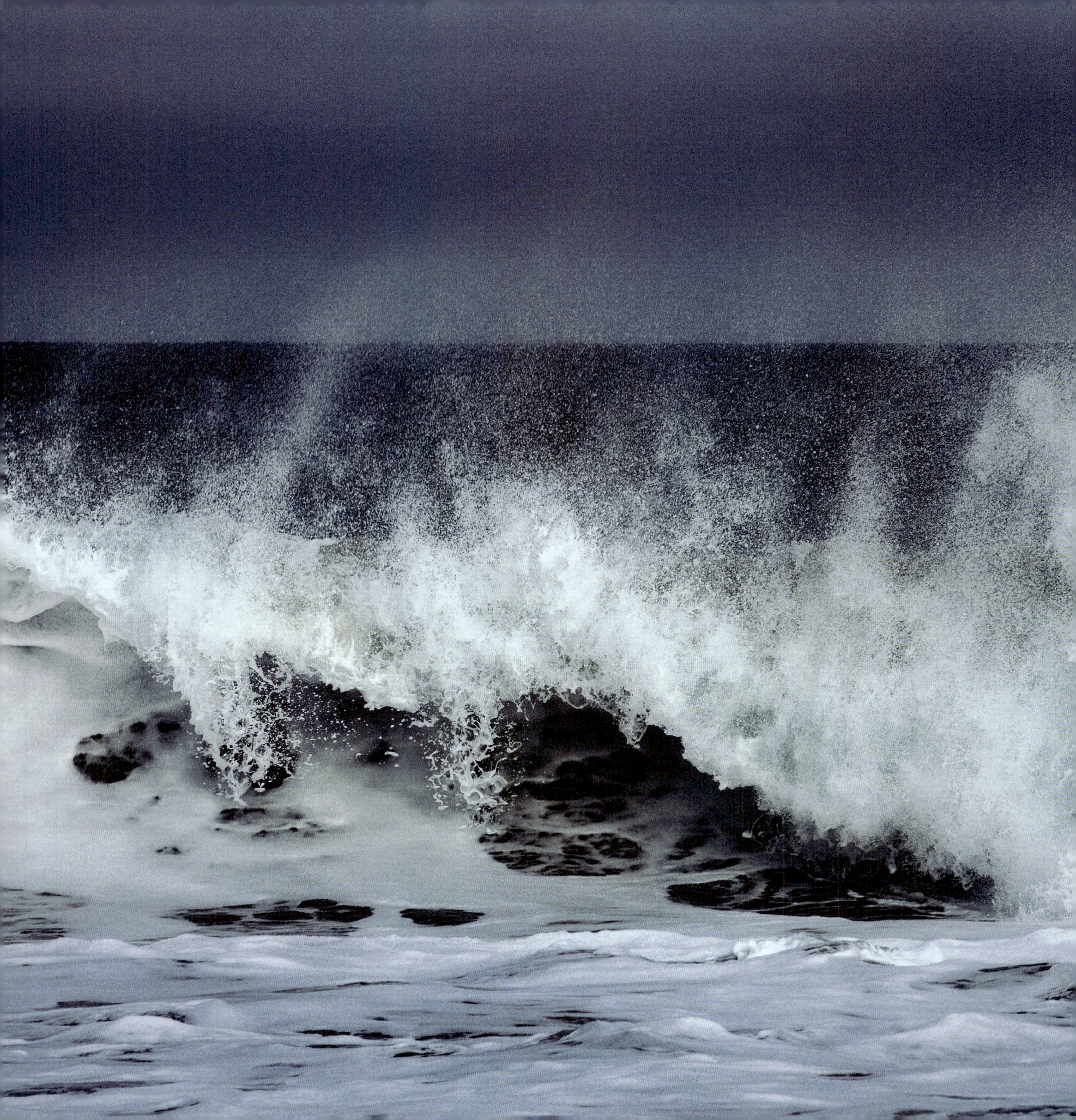

"... it starts off with maybe only four instruments playing ... all of a sudden all sixteen tracks are full." TOM NEWMAN

We'd still have these timing problems and so on, but the performances were what we always wanted to get."

Tom Newman: "The other thing that came out was the way a piece of music is formed dynamically. I mean, it starts off with maybe only four instruments playing, then nine minutes in, there's a little mini-climax and all of a sudden all sixteen tracks are full.

"Because the climax is achieved by adding more instruments to a particular section, after the nine minutes all the tracks are suddenly used and in fact you've run out – so you have to start bouncing down little bits from one track to another in order to gain tracks. Then there'll be another bit where maybe it drops down to only seven or eight tracks, but there's another climax coming on later where again it gets more and more and more. So you've got all sixteen tracks plus an extra load mixed down.

"Michael wanted to do things quickly, and once he got it in his head you had to get it down onto tape. So the particular instruments never seemed to end up on the tracks that they matched. For instance, the first climax might have some guitar parts, but they wouldn't be on the same track as the guitar parts on the next climax. So when it's time to mix it, the problem is you've got to know where all these parts are. There were no computers at the time and we had to do it all by hand. We had this enormous track list that was about 10 feet long – it was so long that it hung over the end of the mixer."

Simon Heyworth: "You had to fill it out by leaning on the floor and writing in the next bit: 'Where does this bit end?' 'Well, it ends sort of there.' And we'd draw these lines: 'Yeah, but the guitar ends there and the piano meets there, so that's really complicated because that means you've got to drop it on track four, but we can't do that because the guitar has got to come in on track four further down the road', and so on.

"So there were all these complications, trying to remember what you'd got and remembering to drop out at the right point, otherwise you'd rub something out that was already there. We didn't have counters on the mixer, so it was always up to one person, normally me, at the tape recorder: 'You've got to drop out NOW, and you've got five seconds left'. And if he carried on playing, I had to drop out anyway."

Tom Newman: "As there was no remote control, any dropping in and out had to be done from a command from the mixer to poor old Simon."

Simon Heyworth: "I became fearless in the end. It was the best training I ever had. And Tom used to rub things out constantly ..."

Tom Newman: "Absolutely, I got credited on a couple of albums as being Tom 'Bulk Erase' Newman. I would quite happily put the whole sixteen tracks into record accidentally and wipe everything out! It was good fun."

Of course, as well as being the place where Simon and Tom worked, it was also the place in which they were living.

Simon Heyworth: "I often wonder about the whole concept of The Manor as a place to be and live. It seems to me that we just loved having lots of old cars. We used to try and fill the drive with as many old cars and trucks as possible. That seemed to be crucial to the whole atmosphere of the place. We had lots of other things going on, we had varied interests; it was almost as if everything else was a little bit more important that actually recording, although we did that 24 hours a day."

Tom Newman: "Yes, it's an interesting thing. The industry has changed a lot, it's got very serious, but back then there was enough pioneering spirit going on, because it was a specialised and a completely different idea. The Manor was the first residential country studio. As such it was a try-on, because nobody knew exactly how to do it, because there was no precedent. And so what it really depended upon was the fact that we could create this community feeling. Everybody who came ended up liking it."

Simon Heyworth: "Oh, it was our home! We had all our personal things around and all our interests – we were all into aeroplanes and cars and if you wanted to find Tom he'd be in the garage, or if you wanted to find me I'd be out with the dogs or something like that. There were always other things going on and I think that was crucial. It was a lovely atmosphere. Even during the building of it, when we were pulling the place apart, everybody who came down there became a part of it. And I think it brought out a lot of good personality traits in a lot of musicians."

Tom Newman: "That's absolutely right."

Simon Heyworth: "They were able to feel comfortable and not pressurised by anything."

Tom Newman: "I'll never forget the end of the building work, putting in the final touches before the equipment was installed, when we used to play 'Sticky Fingers' really loud through these enormous BBC monitors. It was wonderful and I think the atmosphere that was created by the people who were building the place carried right through, at least for the next four or five years."

But the atmosphere was not always calm and happy, as both men will testify.

Tom Newman: "You could blow the whole session if you dropped something in on the wrong bit. If the guitar player had just done a wonderful solo and it hadn't been recorded, there would be trouble. And it used to happen."

Simon Heyworth: "Sure it did. Either it used to happen because I hadn't dropped in and I thought I had or I'd dropped in the wrong track or the signal hadn't been sent to me in the first place."

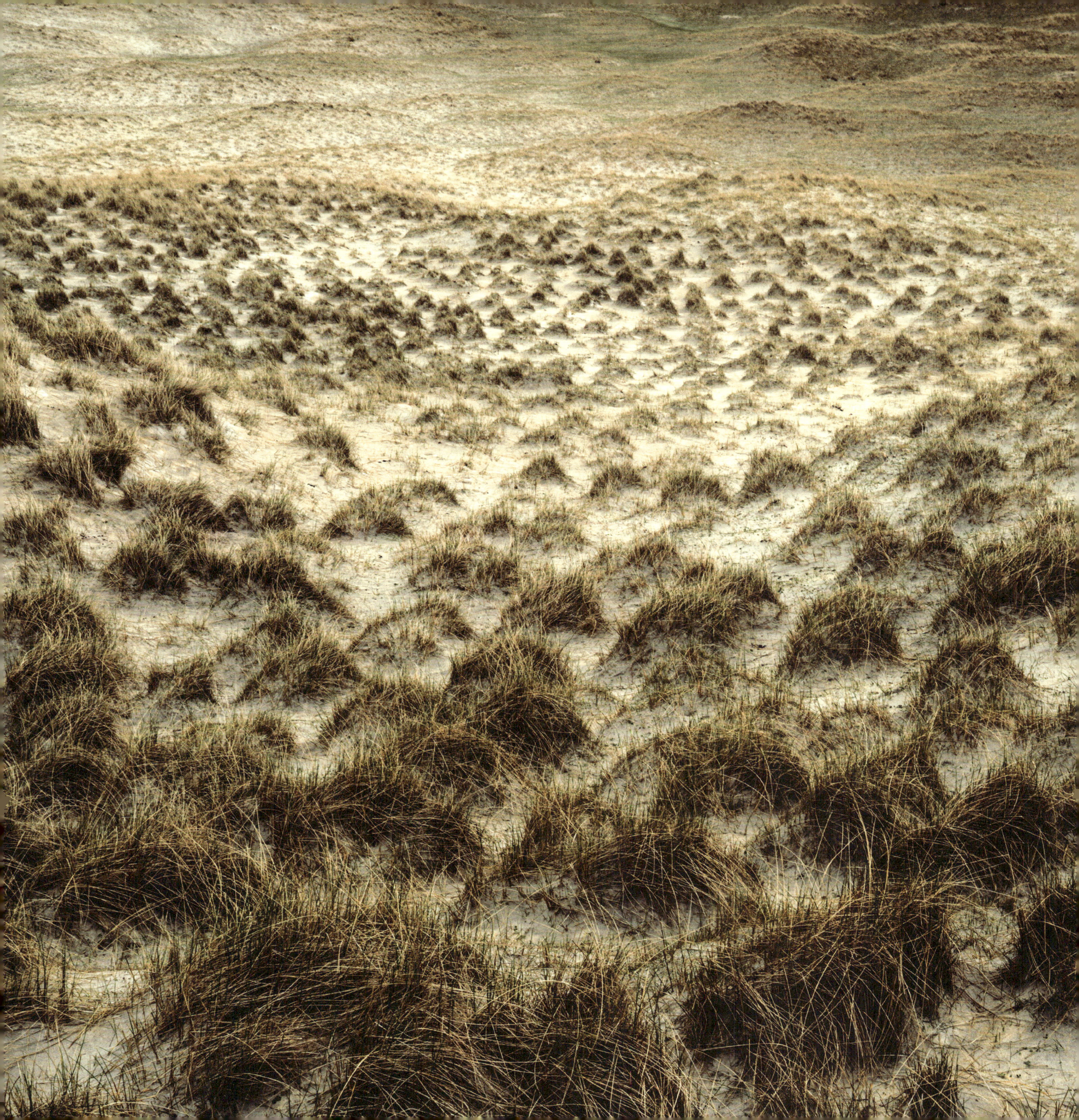

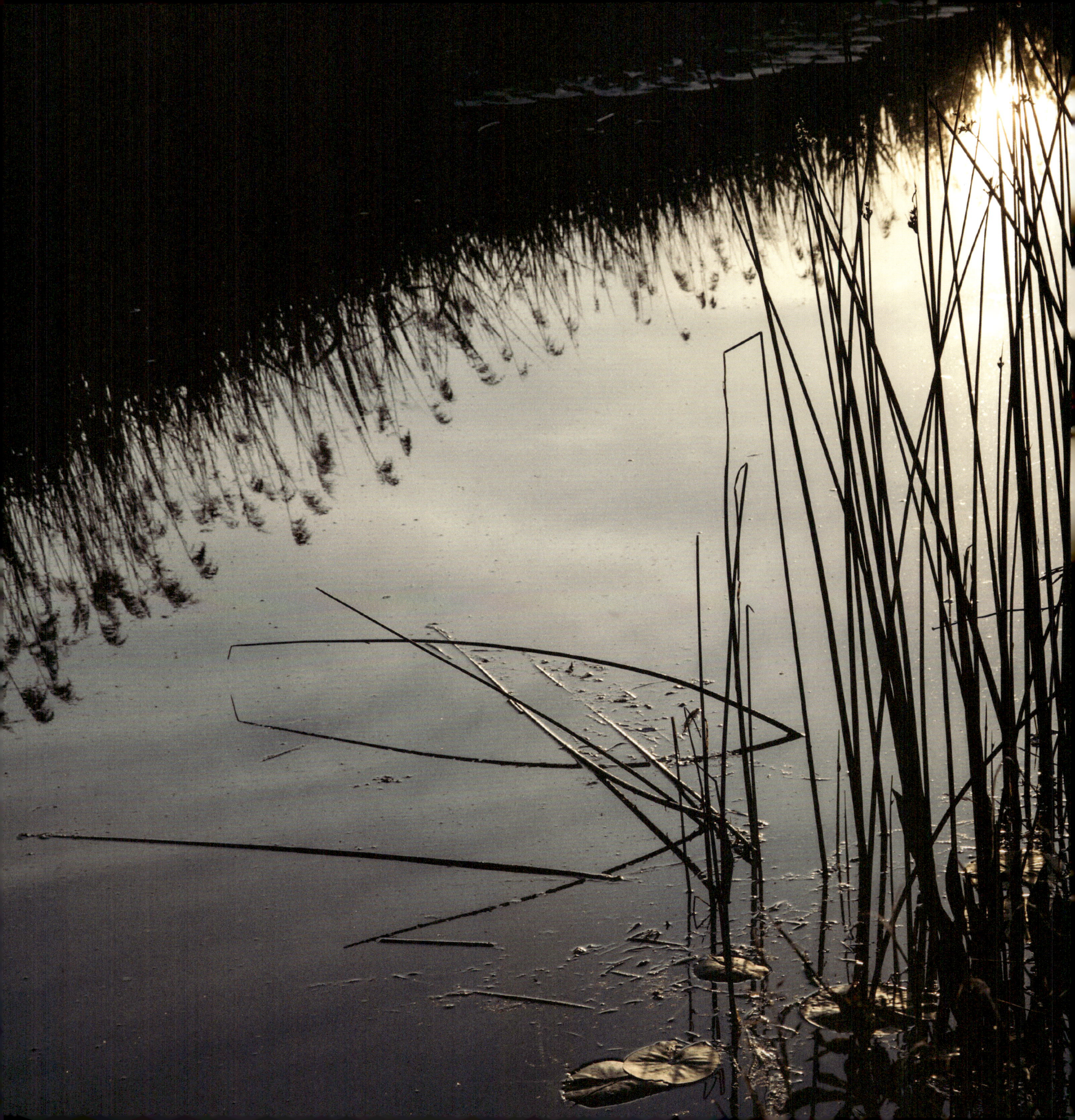

"There are certain little formatted rituals that one develops in the studio, that become a little language, that allow a sense of communication." TOM NEWMAN

Tom Newman: "Absolutely! It was a very disjointed way of recording, because the engineer had no direct contact with the tape recorder except via the tape operator. So it was a very good way of learning very quickly what not to do – and how to undermine the technician if you wanted. But with Michael, because we had to do the whole of the first side in one week, it was a very intense piece of work, struggling through trying to get this great volume of work down onto tape while trying to keep it as unmuddled as possible. Eventually, having done the first side, everything else seemed as if it would flow on nice and simply."

But what actually happened was that the second half of 'Tubular Bells' had to be recorded using time snatched from here and there.

Tom Newman: "Mike lived at The Manor while we were doing other commercial sessions and every time there was an opportunity he'd come in and do a night or a day, whenever there was a break in recording. During this time I was also meant to be the manager and carry on the general business of the studio. But there were times when I wasn't even there. Simon started taping the sessions with Michael and eventually did quite a lot of the recording of side two, and some of the mixes as well. He did several very good mixes of the Caveman song."

A language developed between Tom Newman and Mike Oldfield which allowed them to communicate ideas about the music during recording.

Tom Newman: "It was part of Michael's character that there was a set of tapes that we played to each other; I don't mean real tapes, but mental tapes. There are certain little formatted rituals that one develops in the studio, that become a little language, that allow a sense of communication.

"There were phrases and sayings that were probably leftover from the Bonzo Dog sessions that we would use to mean 'That's great' or, 'I don't know about that' or, 'Yeah, maybe try it again'. So there was a language and a communication that very much centred on the musical, the job to be done, to the exclusion of practically everything else.

"In the evening we would usually have a break around dinner time because there would only be one meal a day, apart from breakfast. Our energies would flag at a certain time, so that would be when dinner was served. Usually after dinner we would go down the pub and get drunk and walk back at closing time and go straight into the studio and carry on with something. There was a local pub very close to The Manor studios which was on the canal which ran by the bottom of the grounds. It was The Jolly Boatman and it was run by Pat and Tony.

"So we would carry on after the pub and sometimes it would be all right if there was a sense of pressure, as there was towards the latter part of side two. We got most of side one done in the one week, buy we didn't get to the very end. In any case there was a biggish gap of a week or two between the first bulk of recording and the next bit. The recording of side two was done sporadically and we didn't get another lump of time until mixing. We managed to wangle three days to mix it in.

“

I’ll never forget the end of the building work, putting in the final touches before the equipment was installed, when we used to play ‘Sticky Fingers’ really loud through these enormous BBC monitors. It was wonderful … . TOM NEWMAN

"We had a few days where we recorded the first lump of side two and then there was a gap. Then Steve Broughton came in and did the drums on the Caveman song. But it was all very hotchpotch, snatching time when we could, the odd day here and there. Michael stayed at The Manor during that time and was ready to come in whenever he could, or whenever there was time."

'Mixing', for those who don't fully understand the term, is when all the recorded tracks are balanced against each other: respective volumes are set; each instrument's apparent distance from the listener is chosen, using echo and reverb; and their position within the stereo landscape is decided upon – either left, right or somewhere in between. When all this – and much more – has been done, the mix is recorded from the multitrack machine onto a stereo 'master'. Due to all the dropping in and multilayering of different tracks, 'Tubular Bells' proved particularly difficult to mix.

Tom Newman: "It was a bastard to mix. It was hands on everything for everyone: me, Simon, Michael and anyone else who was there. We used to call the girls up and say, 'Can you pull this fader down at this moment?' Sometimes there were three, four or five people at the board all with one job to do, like, 'Turn the echo on when I give the cue.'"

Sometimes Newman would clash with Mike Oldfield over production ideas.

Tom Newman: "There was the lonely bell on side one when it goes, 'dong, dong'.

"There was a whole load of other music going on around that on side one and I thought it would sound nicer if it was like a ship's fog bell in the mist. So we had a time pulling all the faders out so that it was by itself and by adding echo it would sound a long way away. That was my plan. But I had to fight to get that because Michael had a different idea about it. Usually I would suggest things that were over-the-top, partly because I was fired by this sense of the filmic.

"Actually I would have had it even more filmic than it was. Michael had more of a sense of it being classical, so he was opposed to a lot of my ideas because I would rather have seen space and distance and he saw it as half-orchestral. He didn't like things flying about too much, like my idea of introducing all the instruments from one side and panning them across to the other. He didn't like that, and that was funny. It was a whim really, but it was something I fought for.

"But it doesn't really matter one way or the other, when it boils down to it. There were loads of ideas like that. I liked the idea of the stage not being like a static orchestra sitting there, I wanted it to be a scene that had players and ideas and things happening on a stage that was constantly changing. Those kinds of things were really the substance of our disagreements and they resulted in some pushing and pulling in the mixing stages.

"He would say, 'Ugh, I don't like that', and jump up and down, but in a charming way." TOM NEWMAN

"It was very much Michael's baby and he got very petulant if there was too much interference with his ideas. But his lack of ability to communicate generally, his difficulty with communication meant that he would say, 'Yeah, all right', or 'Ooooo ugh', and he went completely to pieces if you tried to force something on him that he didn't like. He would say, 'Ugh, I don't like that', and jump up and down, but in a charming way. But it was very obvious to us when an idea wasn't going to work.

"Side two was recorded under very difficult circumstances because of all the stopping and starting. In fact it was recorded over a period of months."

Simon Heyworth: "I did quite a lot of the work on side two: the ending and all sorts of other things. Then we went back and did some bits of side one, or we tried to."

Tom Newman: "Yes, there was a whole lump on the end which got done again."

Simon Heyworth: "And by that time the tapes were nearly worn out anyway."

Tom Newman: "Oh God, yes!"

Simon Heyworth: "We did have a big problem with that; there was a lot of high-frequency loss after so many passes of the tape across the recording heads."

Tom Newman: "That two-inch tape was still in its infancy really, certainly from the technical development point of view."

Simon Heyworth: "On most recordings the tape would pass through probably a hundred times, but we were probably up to a thousand or more by the time we'd finished 'Tubular Bells'. What with all the winding back and forth and doing things over and over again, the tape was literally wearing out.

"By the end of it, Mike was becoming very, very proficient himself. I shall never forget the energy which he used to put into his playing. That always moved me a lot to see him play because it means so much to him to get it out of his system. He really would try hard and he would dig really deep to make it happen."

Tom Newman: "Yes, he was on the edge of his technique, especially on keyboards, a lot of the time. Because he wasn't at that time a really proficient keyboard player."

Simon Heyworth: "He was a very proficient guitarist but he still had to dig very deep to get this energy which was so specific to his playing style. I think it used to drive him mad and he used to get very upset.

"The other thing I used to love was when we would sit around the fire and he would play; we would go and sit and he would play wonderfully. Actually, those are the times I remember

PHOTO: SIMON HEYWORTH

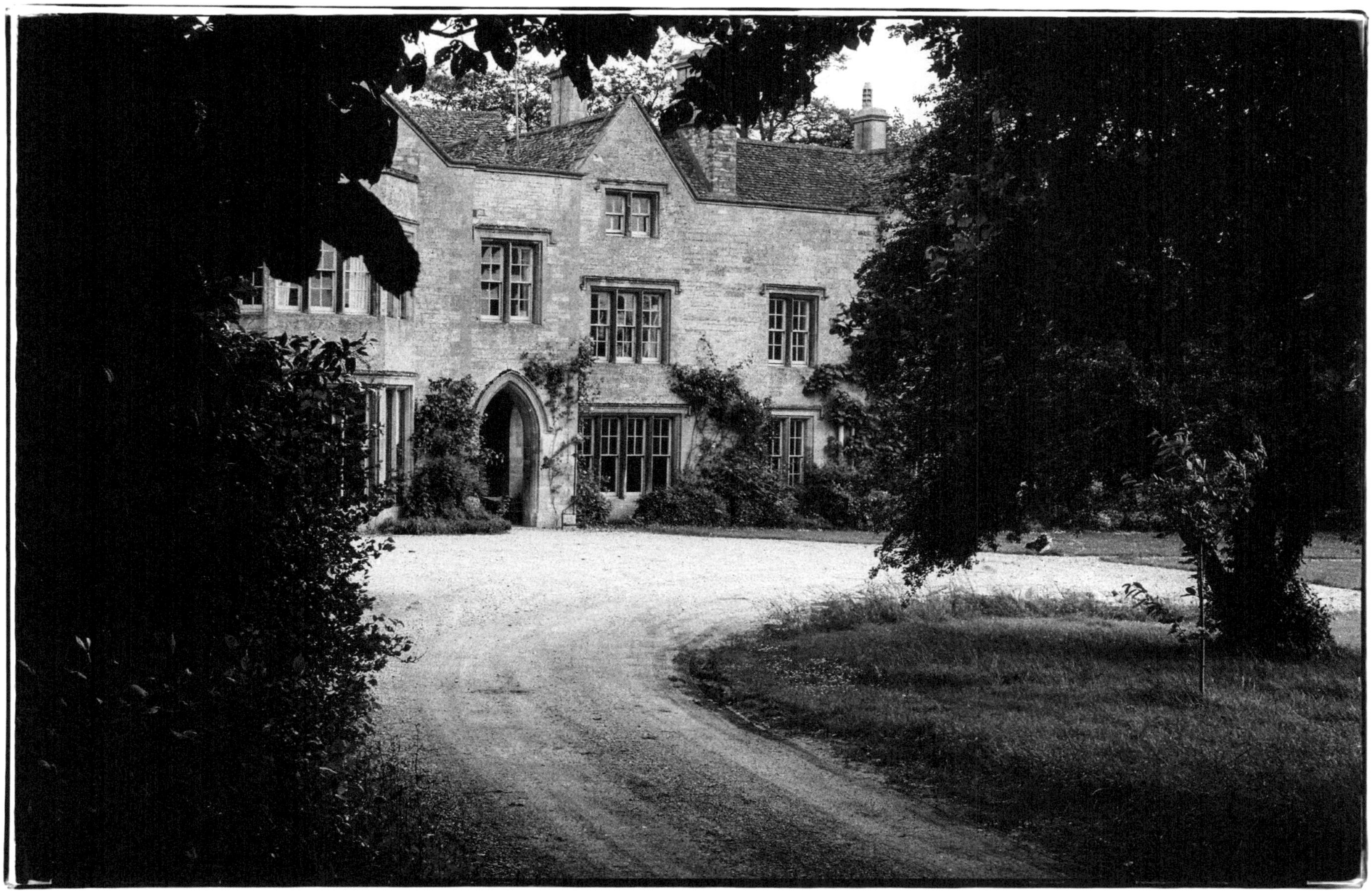

The Manor, Shipton-On-Cherwell, Oxfordshire

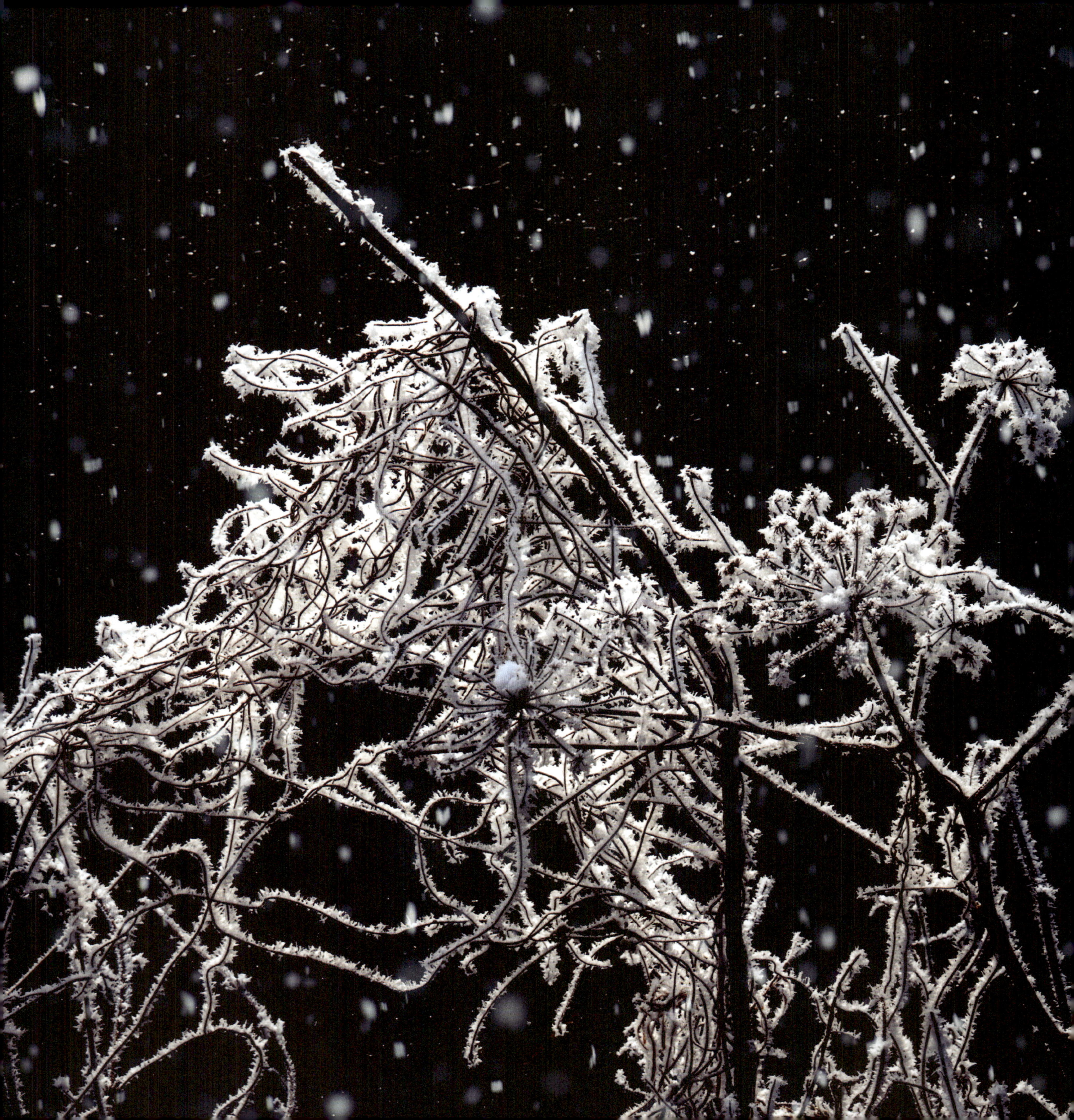

"... we would sit around the fire and he would play ... those are the times I remember in a way more specifically than his playing on 'Tubular Bells'." SIMON HEYWORTH

in a way more specifically than his playing on 'Tubular Bells'. I remember the whole acoustic guitar section very well, but that's just because I'm a great fan of the acoustic guitar and I think that he was a unique acoustic player. When he played just on his own, or with you, socially, then it was fantastic. I'd love to see him do more of that. I always have wanted to, because I think that's where he's really very, very special."

Tom Newman: "The way Mike would start working, I always felt was in a shy way; he was totally unlike other musicians of the day. You would have the standard rock musician whose ego would come in the door a foot in front of him and you'd know exactly what he wanted to do. Michael would just creep in and sidle up the stairs, sit down and look around. The session would start in a way that was much more like two people sitting down and thinking about how to do something. There was no big temperamental artist stuff going on; he was just a very shy, quiet guy who was as confused as the rest of us about exactly how to get this job done.

"And it was a job that he desperately needed to do and it was a case of everybody being in the same boat. What we didn't have was this artist/engineer gulf of hierarchical difference. I felt, and I think we all felt, that we were all in the same little communal boat trying to do this new piece of work.

"Michael would approach the thing in a very unassuming way. We'd start with something and then put the tape on. If it was something we hadn't been doing for a while, he'd usually want to work on some particular bit. We'd get the tape on and he'd listen to it and get a rough balance together. Then we would maybe fiddle with sounds for a little while and then he'd say, 'I want to put some guitar over this bit', and then we were off.

"Once he started recording you had to really be on your toes because it was a continuous flow. You had to very quickly find spaces and know exactly where he wanted to go to. And he'd get upset if you didn't understand what he meant. It's always a problem, communication and the language that you have to develop between yourself and the artist, so that when he says, 'I want to go back to the jiggy bit', you've got to know exactly what he means. It's not like you've got a score; he's not saying 'Go back to letter F' or 'Go back to the beginning of the overture' so you've got this problem where you have to instantly find a rapport between the engineer and the artist."

Simon Heyworth: "We would dictate the best place to go back to for things like drop-ins, because as you listened you'd be sitting there and would gain an ear for these things; you would know that that's where he went out and that's where you had to go back in again. Mind you, I think he'd have got it down anyway, even if he'd been left there alone."

Tom Newman: "I'm sure he would. He firmly believed in what he was doing and there was no reason to doubt him. It's proven by history that the whole thing was absolutely predestined to happen in the way that it happened.

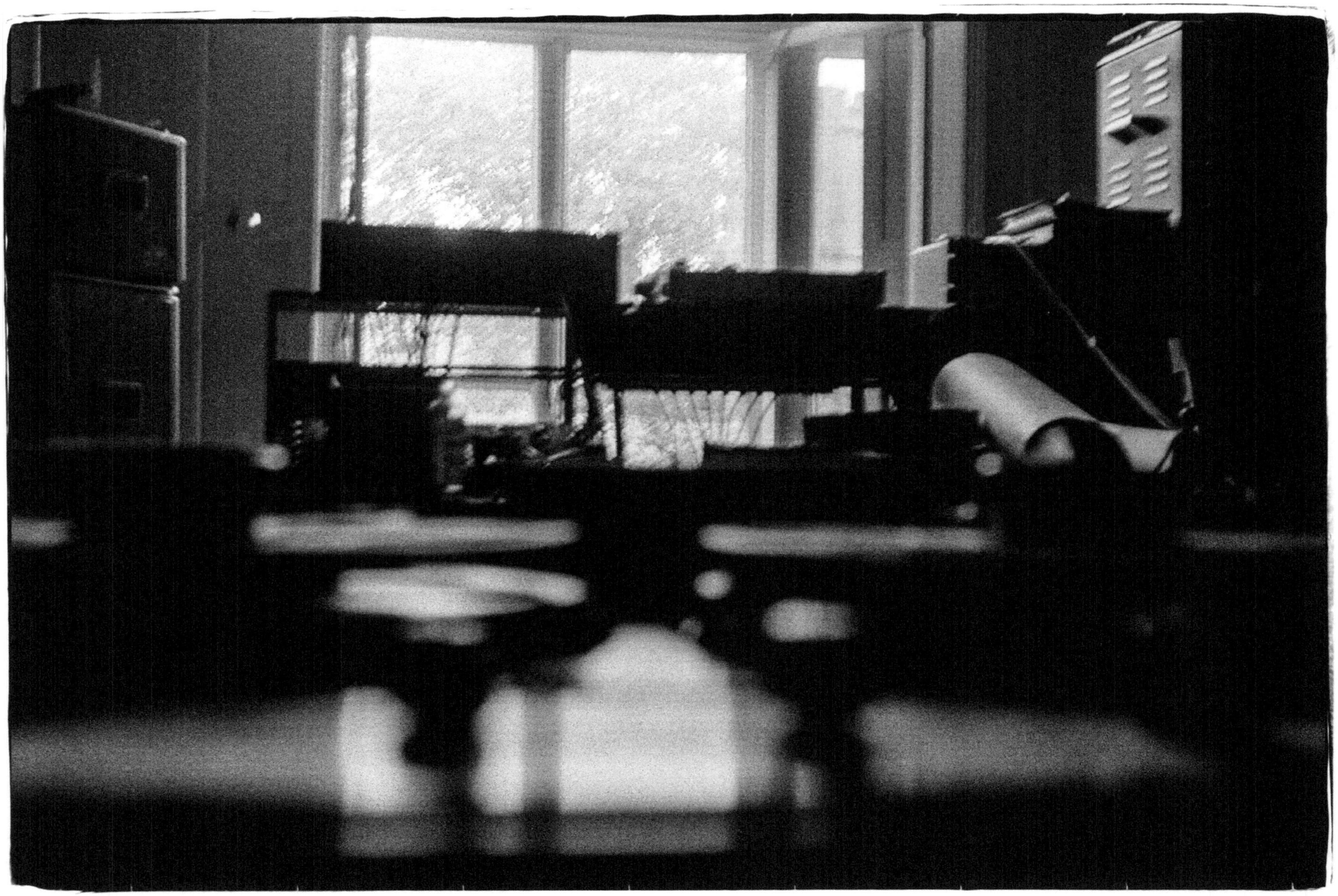

PHOTO: SIMON HEYWORTH

Oldfield's original demo was recorded on a domestic Bang & Olufsen 'Beocord'. It was then transferred onto Ampex 4-track for better quality. This photograph was taken during that actual process.

It was a very magical time, especially the way that the sessions just organically rolled on. What made it organic was that none of us had an absolutely dyed-in-the-wool attitude or idea about what the future held. Whatever happened tomorrow, happened tomorrow. There was no diary, there was no set game plan. Even Richard Branson didn't really have a game plan; he was just busking it in a different way. I'm convinced it was fate and destiny pulling us all together."

Simon Heyworth: "There were so many other things going on as well. We weren't just doing 'Tubular Bells'; Michael's sessions happened in the middle of everything else and we had to cope with the day-to-day running of The Manor and different bands coming in and out."

Tom Newman: "We actually got told off for doing 'Tubular Bells' when we weren't supposed to be doing it. I came back with a flea in my ear from Richard Branson for putting Mike Oldfield in the studio when somebody else should have been in and earning money for him. But once Simon and myself listened to Michael's little demo tape, we both desperately wanted something to happen with the music."

Simon Heyworth: "It was a hit, it was definitely a hit".

Tom Newman: "Actually, I wasn't convinced that it was a hit in its rough form, but it moved me more than anything. Obviously, the thing to do was to talk to Richard Branson, and I remember approaching him about it. I left the tape with him and I don't know whether he listened to it or not, but nothing happened. Then it crossed my mind that it might be better if Simon went to talk to him. So Simon went and had a go at him as well. It's just that Richard really had absolutely no idea about the music. He's got no musical appreciation – I'm not telling tales out of school here; he would admit to that as well."

Simon Heyworth: "He's said it lots of times."

Tom Newman: "The theme from Borsalino was his favourite song and 'Bachelor Boy' by Cliff Richard and that was about it. I don't think it was until Simon Draper came along that there was any progress with the 'Tubular Bells' project."

Simon Heyworth: "Simon Draper was a great ally. He supported us and we got on well with him. He was also starting up the whole idea of a 'label' and signing bands. That was when Virgin actually started. Simon Draper was the one person who was interested in music, but even so it was very difficult to even broach the idea of actually releasing 'Tubular Bells'.

"It was released as a last resort. Their attitude was, 'Well, if nobody else wants it, we've got this mail order catalogue, why don't we put it out?' Then all of a sudden it became, 'Well, we might as well launch the Virgin label with it; if we're to do it, let's do it with this and be really different.' I think that's what captured Richard Branson's imagination, the fact that he was being different and daring, going where no man had been before. It was Richard's sense of gamesmanship."

"I think Virgin were the first record company to release a rock record using a classical pressing." TOM NEWMAN

Tom Newman: "As far as the actual piece of music was concerned, in the beginning it really wasn't Richard Branson who motivated it. It was much more Simon Draper and us that got the project released. Having said that, it's only fair to say that once the whole organisation had been committed to the idea of it, Richard went for it like mad. That was because he'd already committed himself but he was still bucking against the reins because he wanted words on it. He was also worried because there were no drums on it and he was worried because he didn't like the title.

"Richard wanted it to be called 'Startling Breakfast' or something. Then there was the other picture, the rotten egg, which was almost used on one of Mike's later albums, called 'Heaven's Open'. It was an egg in an eggcup which had blood coming out of it – some nonsensical thing. He was really pushing quite heavily and there was a lot of strange friction that had to be got through to actually make the record."

In fact, the friction reached fever pitch when, after continued pressure from Branson and the general difficulty in completing and mixing 'Tubular Bells', Newman and Heyworth decided to deliver it in person – in the form of a barbed practical joke.

Simon Heyworth: "Yes, we decided we were going to let Richard Branson have his record! So, using a discarded mound of 2" tape, which we pretended was the master, we took it up to Virgin headquarters at Vernon Yard and ceremoniously dumped it in the foyer."

When it came to the pressing of 'Tubular Bells' the one instrument which proved almost impossible to re-create effectively was the tubular bell itself.

Simon Heyworth: "In an orchestra the tubular bell is part of the percussion section; it's always regarded as something right in the background and not at all loud. But in 'Tubular Bells' the tubular bells are right upfront and this was always a huge bone of contention between us and Mike, because Mike wanted them loud but we said it was physically not possible to get a tubular bell sounding that loud. You can't have it that loud because it won't cut onto record.

"So the first time we went to cut it, the cutting engineer said to me, 'Simon this just won't cut.' So I said, 'It's got to cut. Widen the grooves, do anything to get it on.' We got it on, but it sounded awful when we heard the test pressings so we had to go back and do it again. Mike used to go mad because the tubular bells were the most important thing. 'I've got to have it loud,' he would say."

Tom Newman: "It must go doon!"

Simon Heyworth: "But it was impossible for it to go doon. We would put compressors on it, but it was never right. The poor old cutting engineers at CBS used to go mad and it was very funny. It was an extremely hilarious part of it. Of course, finally we got it on but it was always very difficult."

Tom Newman: "We got it down partly by keeping the rest of the record down in volume. In the actual cutting it was held down right up until the last doon. We'd give ourselves two or three dBs right the way through so that at the very last minute it could go doon on the doon to keep Michael happy. We'd look at each other and go, doon!"

Simon Heyworth: "But it was good fun."

Tom Newman: "The pressing in fact was a bone of contention; at that time rock records were considered to be dross by the pressing plant so they used to use the vinyl sweepings off the floor. In fact, Richard Branson took great pains, after it became apparent that the only way to keep Michael happy was to have this doon really, really loud, to keep on rejecting test pressings. Eventually Richard went mad at the pressing plant until they used unrecycled vinyl, which was the material they used for classical records. I think Virgin were the first record company to release a rock record using a classical pressing."

Simon Heyworth: "It was a much heavier vinyl."

Tom Newman: "It was actually pitch black as well. It was really good the way it came out and it was the one thing that we fought for to the very end."

Simon Heyworth: "It was the final hurdle before we got there."

Tom Newman: "Doon!"

TUBULAR BELLS

PART ONE

Mike Oldfield plays Grand Piano, Glockenspiel, Farfisa Organ, Bass Guitar, Electric Guitar, Speed Guitar, Taped motor drive amplifier organ chord, Mandolin-like Guitar, Fuzz Guitars, Assorted Percussion, Acoustic Guitar, Flageolet, Honky Tonk Lowrey Organ, Tubular Bells

Master of Ceremonies Viv Stanshall

Flutes Jon Field

String Basses Lindsay Cooper

Nasal Chorus Nasal Choir

Girlie Chorus Mundy Ellis, Sally Oldfield

PART TWO

Mike Oldfield plays Electric Guitars, Farfisa Organ, Bass Guitar, Acoustic Guitar, Piano, Speed Elec Guitars, Lowrey Organ, Concert Tympani, Guitars sounding like Bagpipes, Piltdown Man, Hammond Organ, Spanish Guitar, Moribund Chorus

Girlie Chorus Sally Oldfield, Mundy Ellis

Bootleg Chorus Manor Choir conducted by Mike Oldfield

Drums Steve Broughton (Courtesy Harvest)

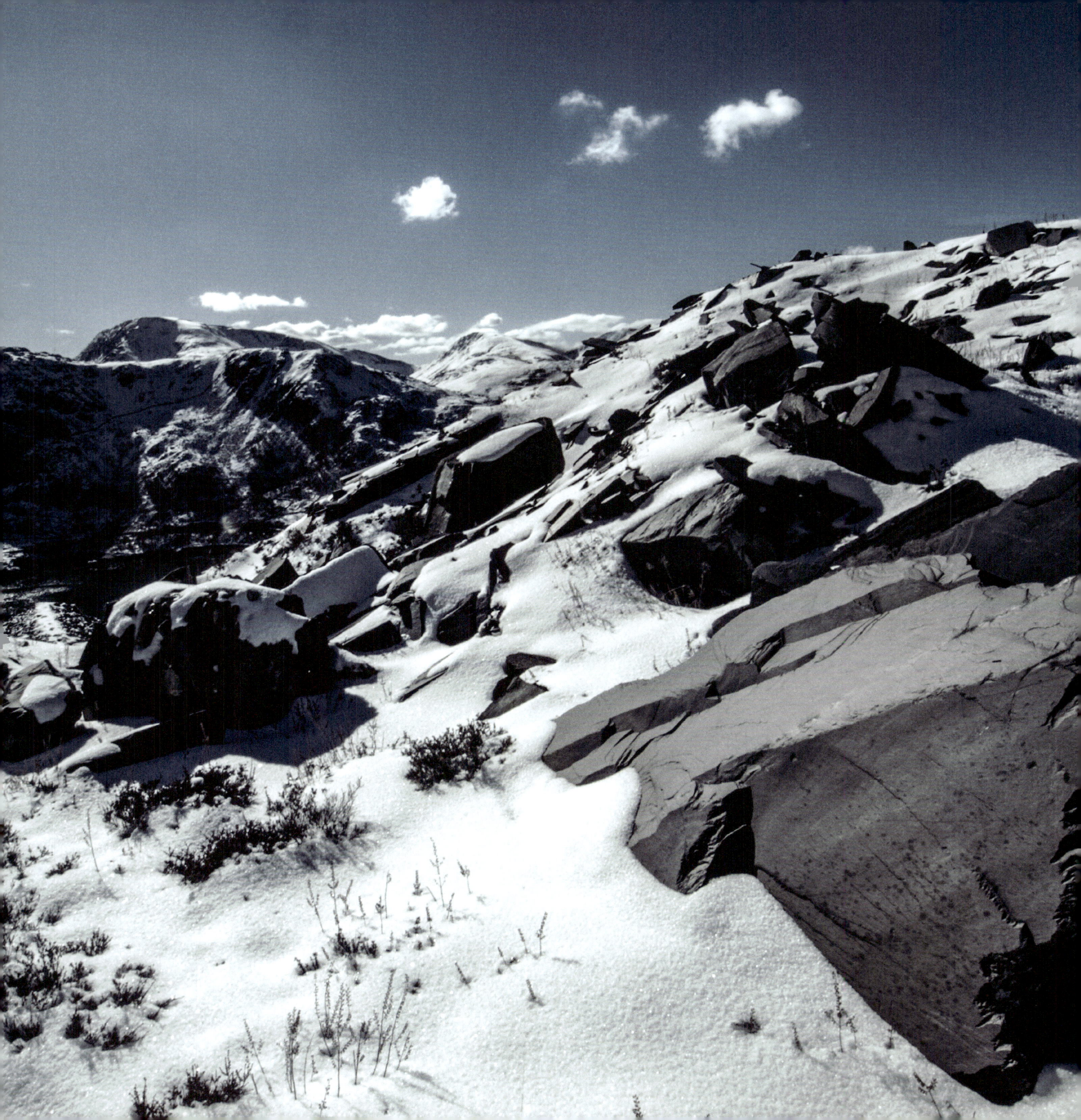

4

POSTSCRIPT TO THE RECORDING SESSIONS

"I*T WAS LIKE dragging stuff uphill through treacle, getting the record released. But once it was out, once it had actually come out, then Richard went mad to do everything he possibly could, in the most bizarre and unprecedented ways, to promote it. The point was that he had no experience. It was rather like us when we were recording it: he had no experience of marketing, therefore he was quite happy to approach it with a completely lateral mind."* TOM NEWMAN

Simon Heyworth: "Richard was very innocent then."

Tom Newman: "Absolutely. And I think that, to be fair, was his forte."

Simon Heyworth: "It was wonderful, especially the concert at the Queen Elizabeth Hall, which of course Mike didn't want to do. I suppose we landed Mike in it by going off and getting it together ourselves. I shall never forget going to Shepperton Film Studios and saying we wanted to hire the stage and we hadn't even got clearance from anybody to do it; we simply went ahead and did it.

PHOTO: SIMON HEYWORTH

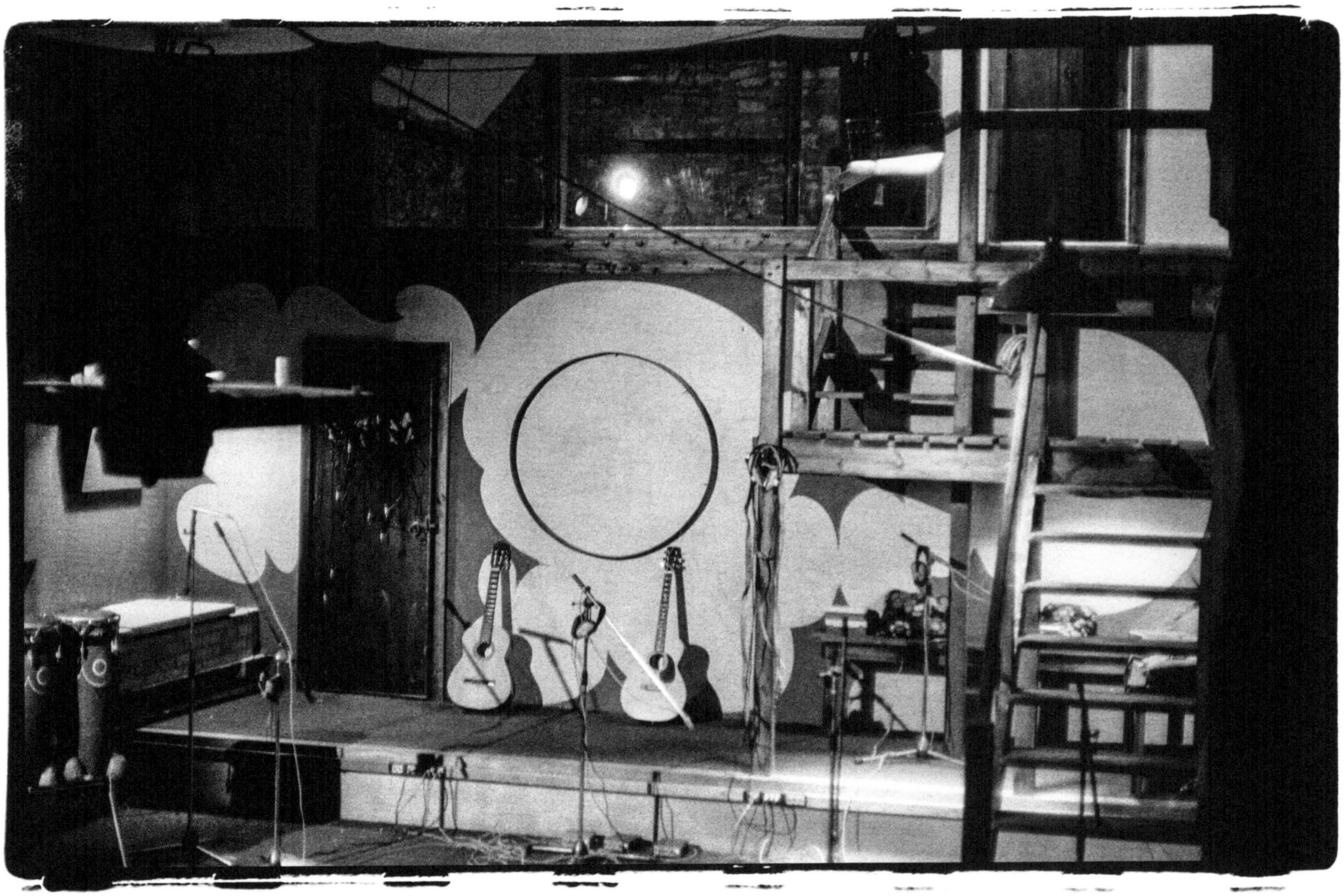

The stage is set

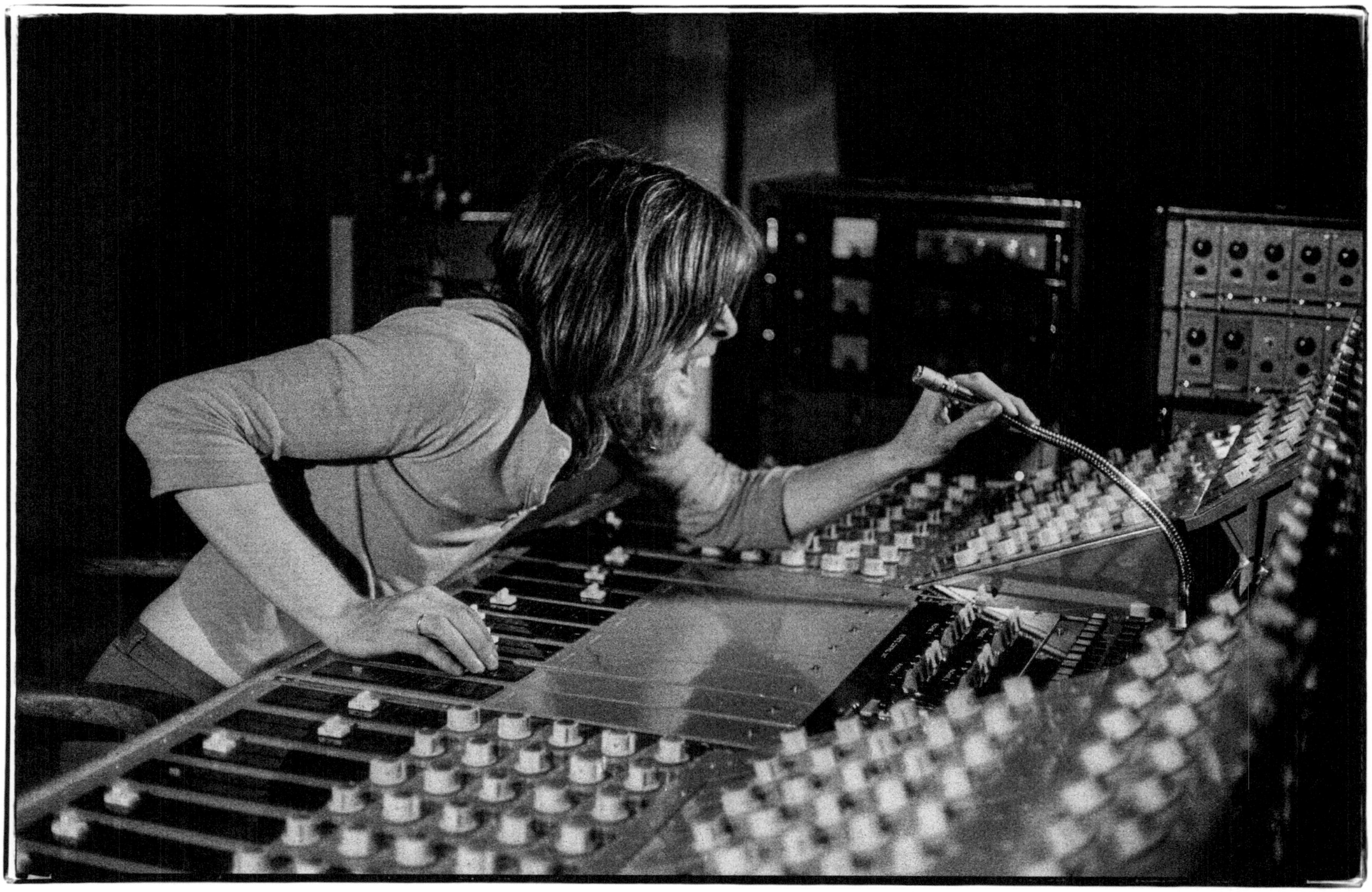

PHOTO: SIMON HEYWORTH

A language developed between Tom Newman and Mike Oldfield which allowed them to communicate ideas about the music during recording.

"We expected something from it, and we got fuck all, not a bloody dicky bird, not so much as a thank-you, not even a postcard from Richard or anybody." TOM NEWMAN

"Again, Simon Draper was the person who we'd go to and say, 'Look, we've got all this together.' And finally it was decided that we were going to do it. Then Richard Branson went and booked the Queen Elizabeth Hall and invited the entire record business, including all the artists as well. Branson did all of that and that was great. The thing that really made it special was his brinkmanship and good ideas and the way he would go out on the edge."

Tom Newman: "The office in London didn't know what was happening down in Oxford most of the time, and yet we were the ones who were actually making the money for them, especially after the record came out and was a massive hit. We couldn't believe it, it was unbelievable.

"We expected an accolade, that there would be some reflected glory, because we'd spent all that time doing it. We cut costs and corners and the whole thing cost, well, nothing really. I don't know what it was written down as, but it was the equivalent to probably two grand's worth of studio time at the current rate at the time.

"We expected something from it, and we got fuck all, not a bloody dicky bird, not so much as a thank-you, not even a postcard from Richard or anybody. We didn't get a wage rise, but all of a sudden Virgin Records is a significant record company and Richard is a millionaire within months of 'Tubular Bells' coming out. We didn't even get a bottle of wine or a pint of beer."

The effect of the success on Mike Oldfield was dramatic, but probably not surprising given his overall state of mind at the time.

Tom Newman: "Michael was flabbergasted, and disappeared almost immediately. As soon as it was out he ran away, because the first thing that happened was that Richard started to pressurise him into doing gigs and the last thing on the planet Michael wanted to do was to go onstage in front of his own piece of work. He'd squeezed this baby out of himself and the birth pangs were by no means insignificant and he wanted to run away. He found it impossible to face the idea of doing a live gig.

"Richard eventually blackmailed him into doing a couple of things, but he hated it; he loathed it. The first thing he did was to buy a house and buy a car and go as far away from society as he possibly could.

"We all had a reaction that was to do with 'Ahhhhhhhh, it's done'. We were so close to it you couldn't get nitpicky about it, whether that bit was a bit loud or whether the tone on that was as good as it could have been. The whole thing had been done under such duress, in terms of the technical, because we were stretching the equipment far beyond its maker's expectations."

Tom Newman did eventually receive some money for his efforts.

"The thing that comes over is that we all had fire in our bellies." TOM NEWMAN

Tom Newman: "I got nothing until the mid-'80s. Then Michael renegotiated his deal with Richard and gave me 1% from then onwards, which gives me between six and eight grand a year, which I am very grateful for. Thank you, Michael, very much!"

For Oldfield to award such a royalty, Tom Newman's contribution to the recording of 'Tubular Bells' must have been significant. Newman assesses it:

"I think, more than anything, I created a workshop feel for Michael to work within. I think he wouldn't have done it in the same way if he had been put into EMI with, say, Geoff Emerick. Now Geoff Emerick is a brilliant engineer and he can hear the effects of 100 kHz on a signal and stuff like that – I've got enormous respect for him – but I know he couldn't have set the scene correctly for Mike Oldfield to bare his soul in the way that he did. It was as much to do with taking him down the pub and getting him drunk on Guinness as it was to making suggestions about having 50 mandolins doing this bit and the hundred pipers doing that bit. They were things that came from me, but they were incidental.

"So it wouldn't have happened without me on one level and I am also sure it's true that everything Michael knows about the mixers and the recording and everything he uses now, he learned from me. At the same time I can't really take a great deal of credit for that because I was only just mastering it myself. It was osmosis, there was an organic learning thing happening; it was to do with the fact that we found ourselves in this situation and we had to learn because there was no other way to do it. We were thrown in at the deep end and we have to survive and make it work. So we learned and we pulled upon whatever gods and whatever forces and whatever powers we could in order to make it work. And fortunately they were enough.

"The thing that comes over is that we all had fire in our bellies. Simon Heyworth had fire in his belly for the project, I had fire in my belly for the project and it was Michael's music that inspired us to (a) use our ears and (b) work on the edge of our respective techniques. Simon's fingers were all over the place; he was rushing backwards and forwards between the machines; I was doing all the editing because I was better at it and we shared all the tasks. Simon put an enormous amount into it; no less or no more than I did, but the way that it worked out was that I had to shoulder the bulk of it because it was my baby to a certain extent. But it wouldn't have happened in the same way without Simon Heyworth. The same way that it wouldn't have happened if it had been someone else's record. Michael's inspiration was there to make it all work."

PHOTO: SIMON HEYWORTH

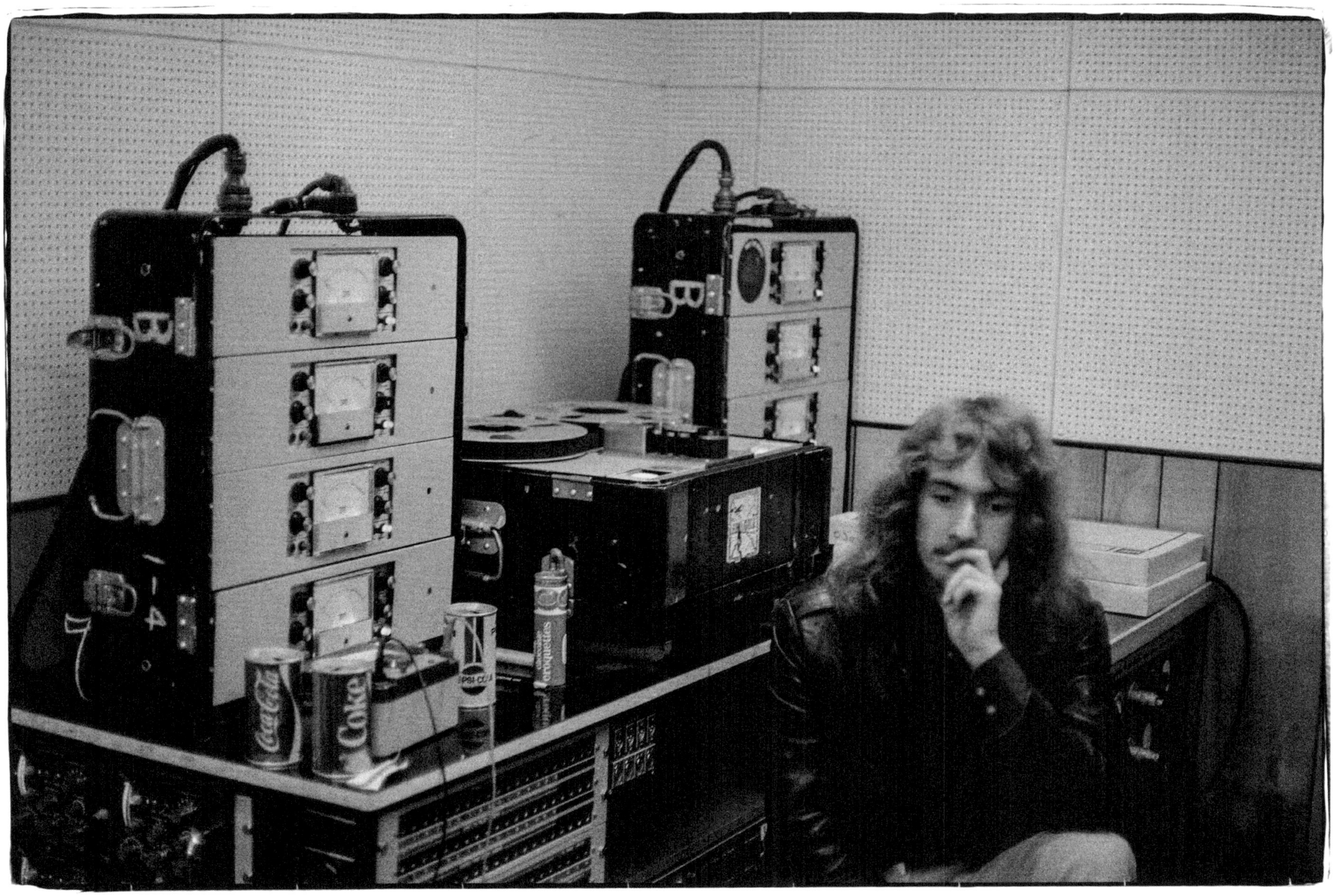

Phil Newell with the tape transport, metering and amplification for his 8-track console

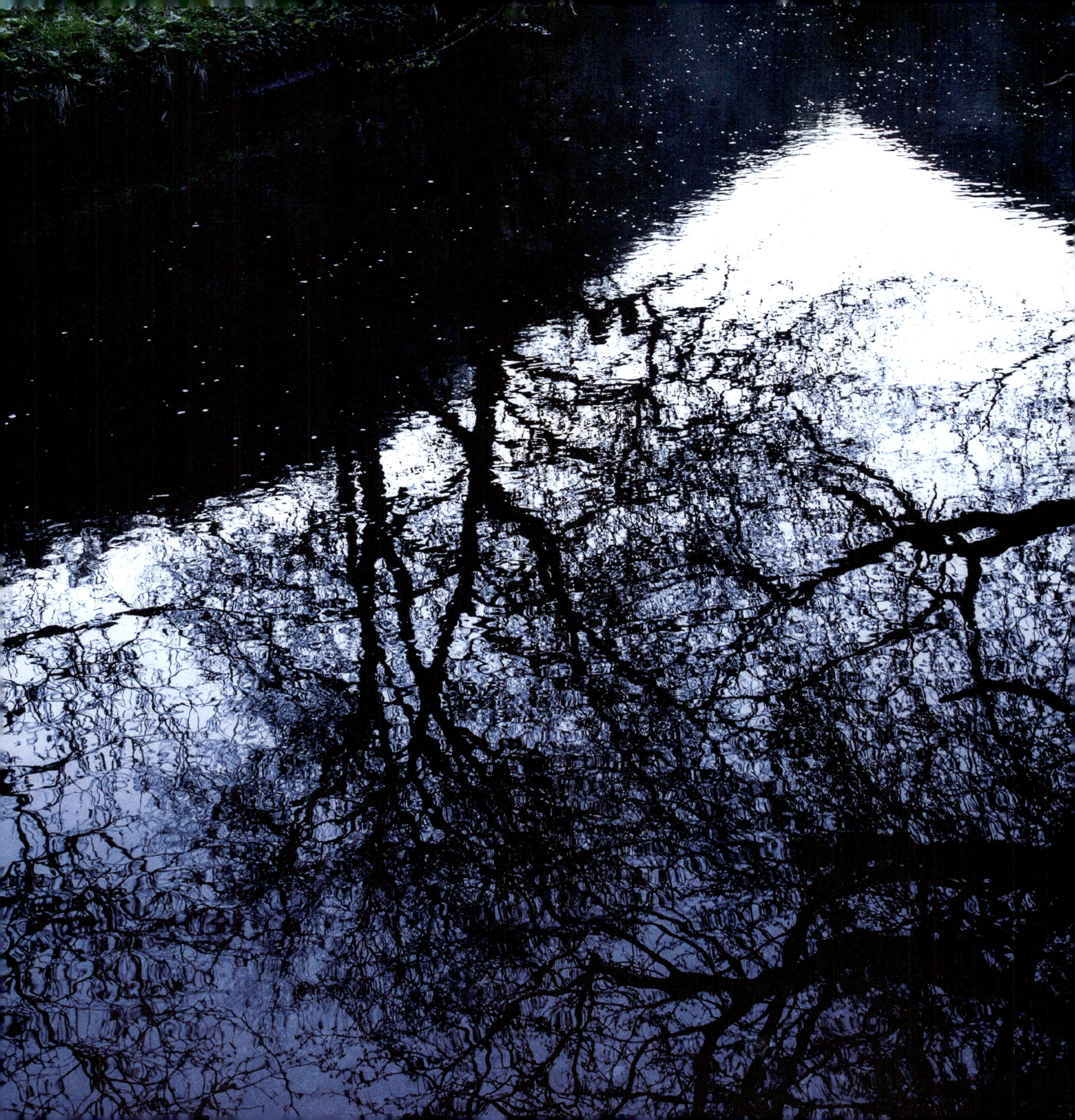

MIKE OLDFIELD REFLECTS ON THE ALBUM WHICH MADE HIS NAME

*“I**t’s more than** 20 years since ‘Tubular Bells’ and while I’ve made a lot of music since then, there is something very special about that album. After I made it I diverged away from it and never really returned to that type of music. I don’t know why I did that, but I suppose I felt that I had completed what I had to say in that musical vein at that particular time.”* MIKE OLDFIELD

Mike Oldfield: “Listening to it now, it still sounds very up to date. I think I’ve still got a lot to learn from it because there were some really good ideas in it – ways of using multiple melodies at the same time, little tiny fast ones up in the real highs, and very slow ones in the bass and maybe other things in the middle. Rather than having a set of chords and a tune, you’ve got multiple things happening, more like a canvas, a painting, a landscape.

“The idea for ‘Tubular Bells’ first came when I was working as a bass player in Kevin Ayers’ group Kevin Ayers & The Whole World. We used to travel up and down the M1 in a Ford Transit. We just happened to be at the same venue as this huge jazz orchestra; it was called Centipede and it was organised by Keith Tippett. That was the first time I had ever seen or heard a long piece of music. It was about 25 or 30 minutes long with all sorts of different styles and musicians – African musicians, jazz musicians, even a rock vocalist. I thought this was a stunning idea, and having listened to and loved classical music for most of my life, but being a rock musician, I just got the idea of making my own electric version of it. I’m loath to call it symphony, but in effect that’s what I tried to make it.”

Eventually Oldfield decided to play all the instruments himself.

Mike Oldfield: “Well, Kevin Ayers & The Whole World were recording at Abbey Road just slightly after the time when The Beatles were there. I used to get into a studio at Abbey Road before the session started. Down in that studio, number two, there used to hundreds of instruments, so I could just get there in the morning and mess about. I found that I could play enough instruments well enough to get the tunes that I needed. I could play tympani, I could play vibraphone, and there was an old set of tubular bells there and different pianos, organs and all sorts of things. It was like an Aladdin’s cave and I used to go there a couple of hours before the Kevin Ayers sessions started and play about.

“While I wouldn’t describe myself particularly as a multi-instrumentalist, if you give me something, I’ll learn how to play it well enough to make it sound good. I can’t play anything complicated on these things, not like I can on a guitar, but I can make them sound good. I enjoy playing different instruments, which is probably why.

PHOTO: SIMON HEYWORTH

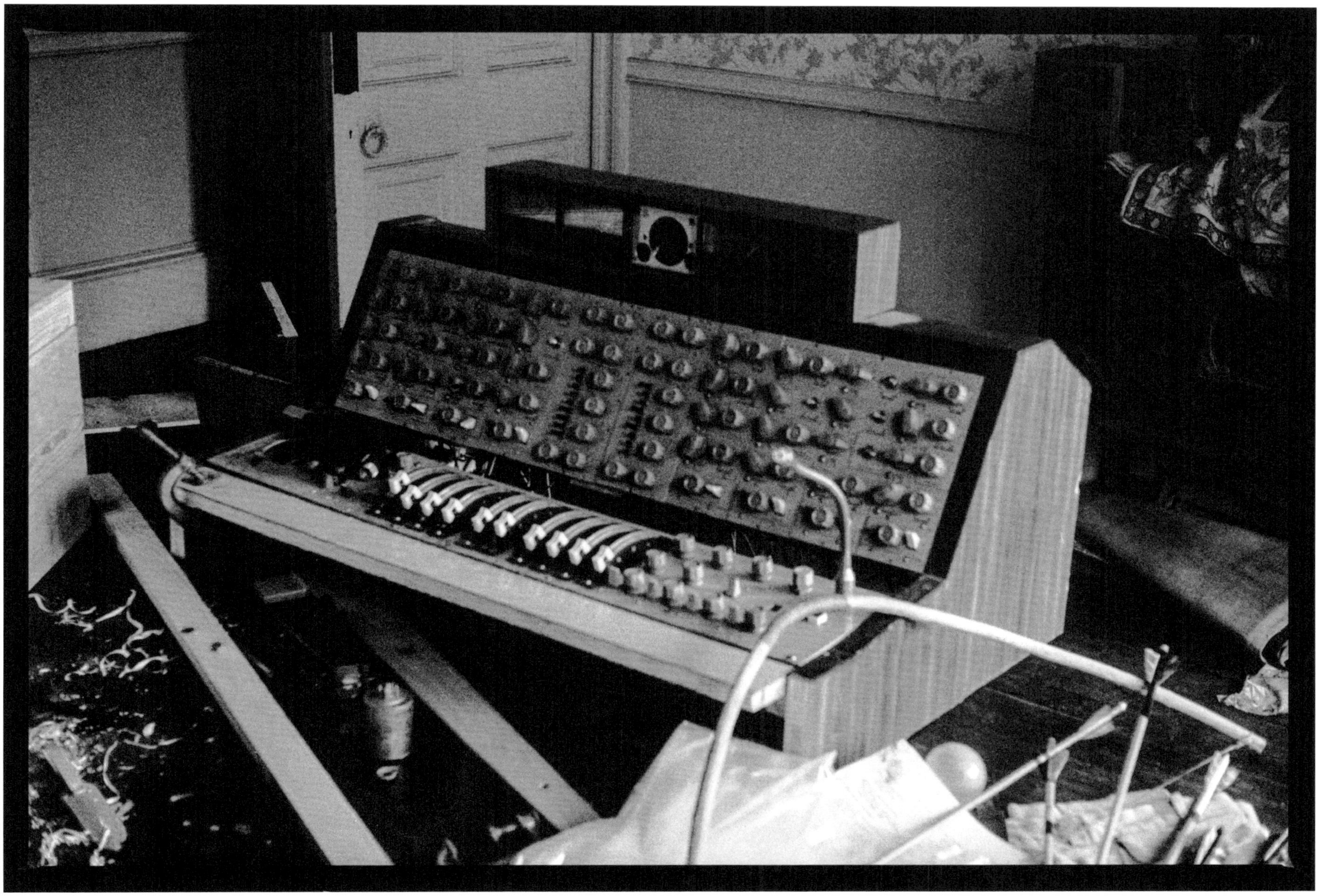

The 8-track recording console was stored at Albion Street until it could be moved to The Manor

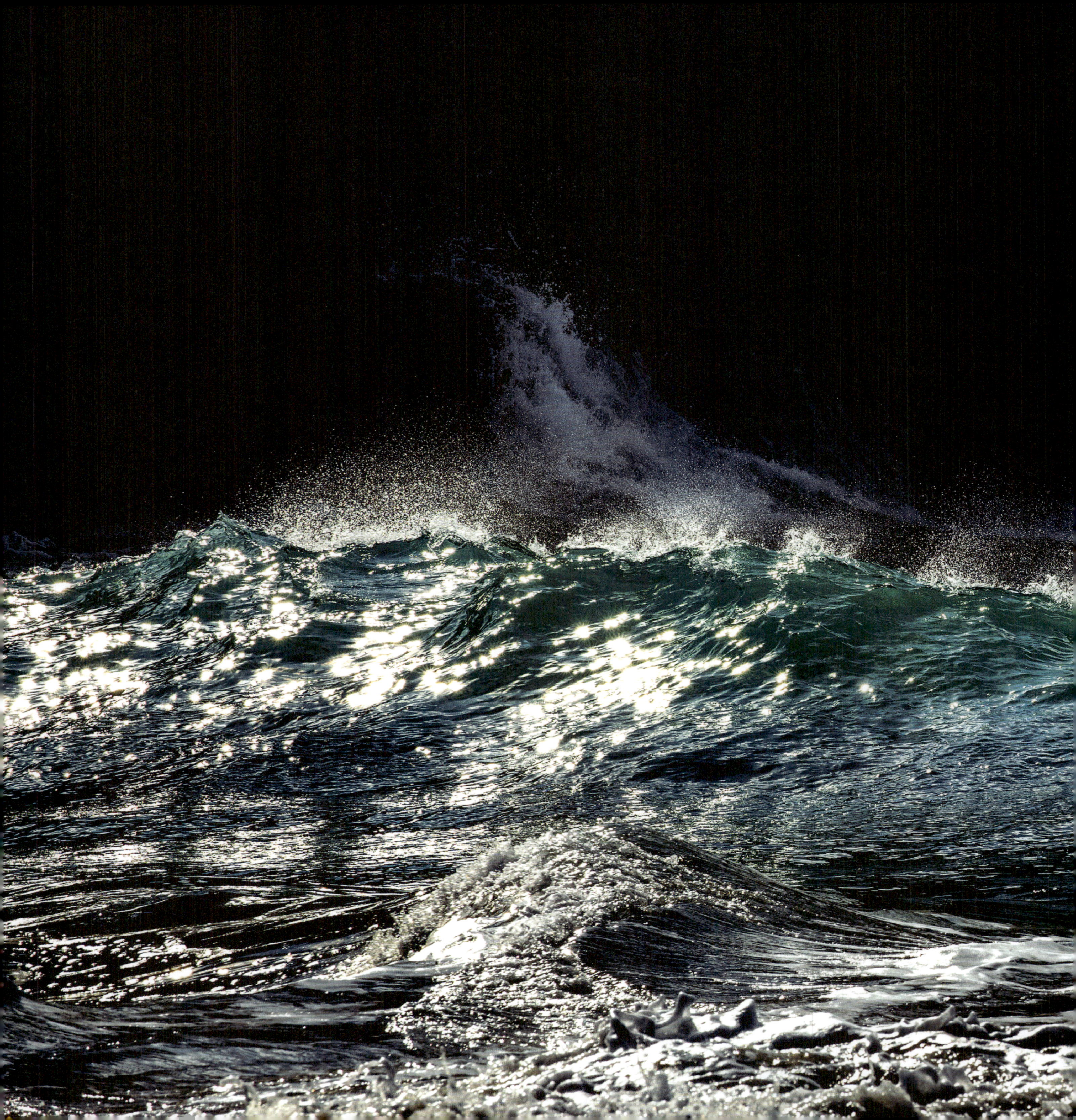

"Then it was as if my dream had come true, to have a whole studio to play with and all the instruments that I wanted." MIKE OLDFIELD

"I first came across Tom Newman at The Manor. After Kevin Ayers & The Whole World split up, I was an unemployed musician for a while. I had various jobs, including rhythm guitarist in 'Hair'. I got the sack because I used to play everything in 7/8 time and the dancers kept falling over to my guitar playing. Then I got a job as a bass player with this other band who were rehearsing at The Manor and we drove down there, although I wasn't really happy with this group. I happened to meet one of the engineers there, Simon Heyworth, and Tom Newman as well. I told them I had some tapes that I'd really like them to hear. They were just building their studio at that time. So I got in my car and went all the way back to Tottenham, where I was living, for my demo tapes and took them back to The Manor and played them to Tom and Simon. They really liked them."

Tom Newman particularly liked the 'Hoover' track, which eventually was left out of the album.

Mike Oldfield: "The only reason there was a Hoover on it was that I wanted bagpipes, which I didn't have. I wanted something that went 'Hmmmm mmmm' and the only thing I could think of was a Hoover."

Having presented his demo tape to Newman and Heyworth, Mike Oldfield was anxious to find out whether or not Richard Branson would be interested in the project.

Mike Oldfield: "I kept ringing up Tom and saying, 'What's happening?' and he told me nothing was happening. I really didn't know what to do. I felt all I wanted to do was to be a working musician to make my music. I thought maybe they would appreciate me in Russia – I'd read somewhere that the Russian Government paid musicians. I remember getting up one morning and saying, 'I give up.' Then suddenly the phone rang, it was Simon Draper and he said, 'Come over and have dinner with me and Richard Branson, we want to talk to you about your record.'

"I went over and had a meal with them and told them the list of instruments that I would need to hire. They gave me a week at The Manor just to see how I did.

"It was a wonderful place, The Manor; it was a big, old stone house with a lovely, great big fireplace and the whole atmosphere there was really exciting. There were a lot of people living and working there as engineers, people cooking, cleaning and the whole thing felt like some sort of great big family. It was very exciting, a lovely place to be.

"Then it was as if my dream had come true, to have a whole studio to play with and all the instruments that I wanted. I remember Tom was late the first day, so that was handy because it gave me the chance to practise everything. Then, when he came in he was a bit hassled, but by the end of the second day the whole thing was sounding so wonderful. When we pressed the 'play' button it sounded fantastic.

"I really lived in my music and was thinking about it 24 hours a day. That's one of the things that makes 'Tubular Bells' so believable. It's got 100% conviction in it." MIKE OLDFIELD

"We worked like dogs for a week. I only had a week, so if I hadn't come up with anything, that would have been it. So I worked like an animal, just to finish the first side. I finished virtually the whole of the first side in a week, apart from one little acoustic guitar piece at the very end. Then we had to mix it, which was a real problem. It was very difficult because of the way I worked – and I still work – in that I have to do something quickly.

"Tom liked putting it down on tape whenever he could. We had 16 tracks of tape and they were all full all of the time, and they were all changing into different instruments as the 25-minute piece progressed. So you'd have your fader up, which is one channel on the mixing desk, and it would be a guitar, and then suddenly it would change into a piano and then suddenly into something else. All the tracks would be changing in the same way. It was a nightmare to make any sense of.

"Somehow we managed to do a rough mix. We were up all night doing this mix and we gave it to Simon Draper and he loved it. Then there was a very quiet period after that, because I think they had to rent out The Manor because they needed the money. And although I stayed on for a little bit I had to leave in the end. Various bands came in and out and worked at The Manor. The arrangement I came to was that I would live in The Manor and whenever anyone wasn't using the studio, I would nip in and use it. So it sometimes meant working at night and sometimes in the morning. Sometimes I'd get a week or a few days here and there and gradually I worked up and did side two. I did it like that in lots of little bits and pieces."

During the time of the recordings Michael's mental state was not good.

Mike Oldfield: "I was in a very insecure frame of mind at that time. I had problems with my family and the time I'd spent with Kevin Ayers wasn't very happy and I was probably having a nervous breakdown. That's the way I would describe things around the time of 'Tubular Bells'.

"At that time the music was so important to me, more real than normal reality. I really lived in my music and was thinking about it 24 hours a day. That's one of the things that makes 'Tubular Bells' so believable. It's got 100% conviction in it. And I still have that conviction.

"For the whole of the recording I was in a desperate panic, because I only had a week and there was such a lot to do and the music was going to last 25 minutes. On the very last night I could see that time was ticking away. Everything – even the tubular bells – was done in a rush, because the Bonzo Dog Band were waiting to come in the next morning.

"I suddenly had an idea. The finale of side one has all the instruments appearing one after another and I got the idea to ask Viv Stanshall, of the Bonzo Dog Band, to come and introduce them. He came in and I pointed at all the instruments and he'd say, 'Grand piano, tubular bells ...' etc. Then he went out again and that was that.

PHOTO: SIMON HEYWORTH

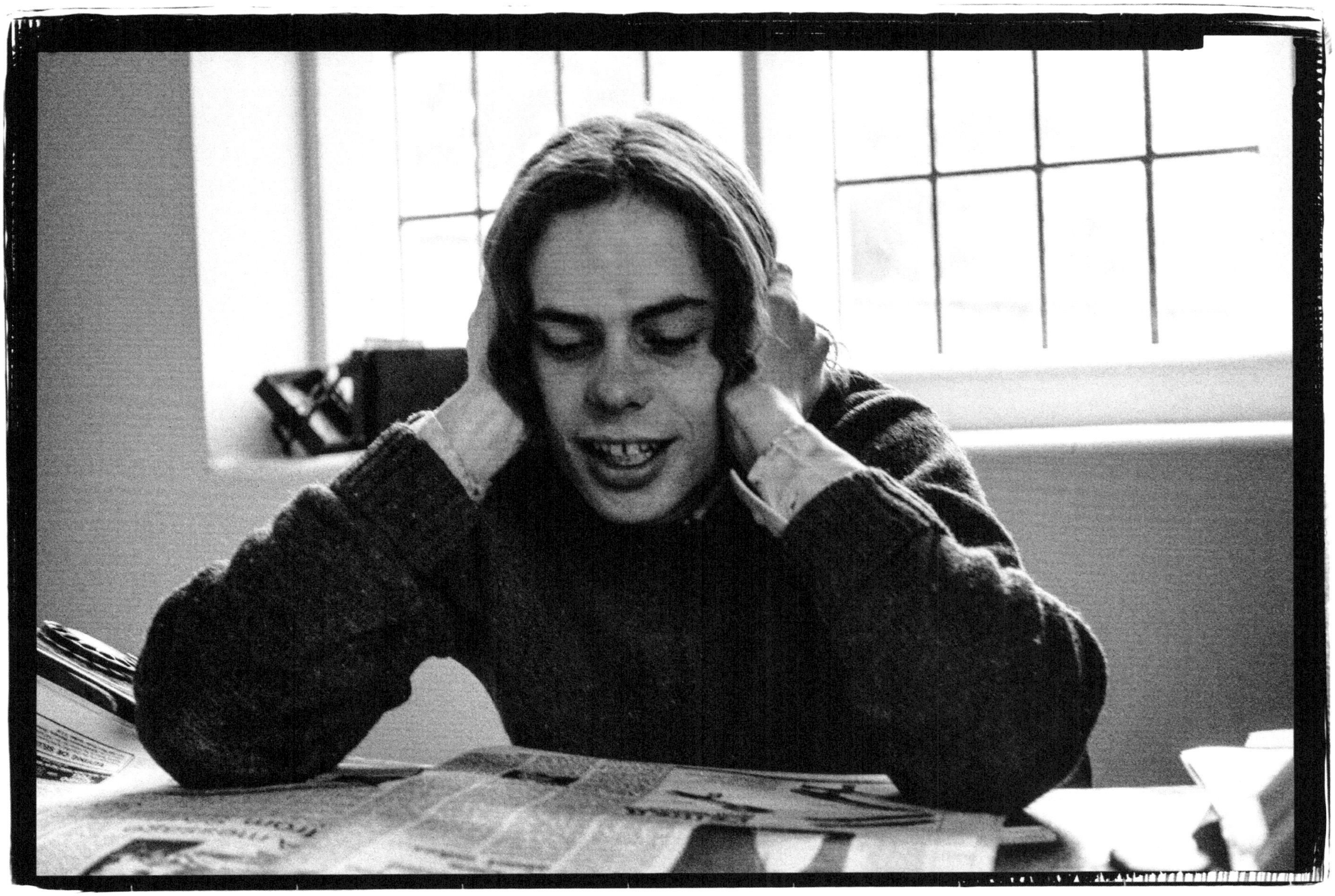

Simon Heyworth

"So I said, 'Can I have your Bentley?' It was a bloody silly thing to ask, because he gave it to me and I didn't realise it was totally clapped out!" MIKE OLDFIELD

"After it was all finished Richard Branson and Simon Draper decided I was going to do a concert. But I didn't want to because, having gone through the recording and mixing of 'Tubular Bells' the idea of a group of people sitting and playing it seemed ridiculous. It was such a complicated mix.

"I remember them spending a whole afternoon in a room at The Manor, bullying me, cajoling me and trying to persuade me that I had to do a gig. In the end I think I said something to Richard like, 'What do I get if I do it?' He said, 'What do you want?' I always liked his Bentley, it was a really nice car, and he would come swishing into The Manor with his beautiful wife Kristen in his Bentley. So I said, 'Can I have your Bentley?' It was a bloody silly thing to ask, because he gave it to me and I didn't realise it was totally clapped out! You got in it and your foot went through the floor. The whole car was falling to pieces underneath. I took it to a garage and they said it would cost more to fix than it would to sell it.

"Anyway, I was 19 and I agreed to do the concert. There was more work in organising the live gig than in recording the record. First, if all I had to write out the parts for 12 or 15 musicians. I'm not brilliant at writing music, but I had to sit and write the whole thing out. That took ages and then I had to find the musicians and teach them how to play it.

"It was much easier when I was playing everything. It's difficult trying to explain to a guitarist how to play something because we all play differently. But anyway, I had agreed to do it so I organised it and did it. But I was completely terrified at the thought of performing it in public. We rehearsed at Shepperton Studios. Also, we had Mick Taylor, who was The Stones' guitarist, in the band. I always thought he was very unusual because he used to drive around with a woman chauffeur in a Mercedes and he'd wear a snakeskin suit! I thought that must be so itchy.

"So we got to the Queen Elizabeth Hall and I was sitting in the dressing room and people were coming in. I always remember Mick Jagger sitting there in the dressing room with me. He came with Mick Taylor and I remember him being really supportive. I can't remember what he said but he really calmed me down.

"We went out and did the gig and as soon as I started playing I was just concentrating on what I was doing. I was conscious that it wasn't sounding right. It just didn't sound anything like it should and Viv Stanshall introduced everything in the wrong place. He introduced the piano in the tubular bells place, and the tubular bells about a minute and a half after they had finished playing. It was a disaster! We got all the way through side two and at the end I was thinking, 'Just take me home', because it had been a total disaster.

"After the concert 'Tubular Bells' gradually took off. I must say, before I even made it, I just knew that it was going to be very successful." MIKE OLDFIELD

"I had my eyes shut as I was expecting to get pelted by tomatoes and bananas. But I opened my eyes and the entire audience was standing. I'd never seen a standing ovation. I was staggered because I thought it was so awful and they obviously thought it was so great. Then along comes Richard Branson and he wants to lift me up on his shoulders and parade me round the bloody theatre. I was fighting him off and saying 'Get off!' So that really was confusing.

"After the concert 'Tubular Bells' gradually took off. I must say, before I even made it, I just knew that it was going to be very successful. It wasn't an egotistical thing; I just had this really strong feeling that people would like it because I believed so much in it myself.

"With regard to the original theme for 'Tubular Bells', what happened was this. I'd had a bit of an argument with Kevin Ayers because I felt that I didn't want to be in a group anymore. But at that time I was really carrying the group; my bass playing was very important for that group and my guitar solo had become a part of what the audience expected to see. So when I left, they tried doing gigs but people complained that I wasn't there anymore.

"So we tried getting back together again and it didn't work. Anyway, Kevin agreed to lend me his tape recorder, which was only a two-track machine. But I love fiddling with bits of electronics, even though I'm hopeless at it. I usually end up destroying things, but I like getting a screwdriver out and taking things to bits and I managed to work out a way in which I could do stereo overdubs on this two-track machine, involving sound on sound. This was putting one track down, bouncing it to the other track and then adding something. If I blocked off the erase head with a bit of cardboard, I found I could put another couple of things on the tape, so you got this stereo picture. I had all this set up in my bedroom in Tottenham, where I also had an organ.

"A couple of things were popular at the time. One of them was 'A Rainbow in Curved Air' which was the music of this guy called Terry Riley. It was a sequence of music, but it was hand-played, because there weren't any sequencers back then.

"The music was very repetitive but Kevin was always trying to interest me in it. I would say, 'Wasn't that a bit repetitive?' and he would say, 'Yes, it's supposed to be'. As a concept it was repeating something over and over again, and at the time I thought it was a bit pointless, but then I began to see a meaning in it – it's not out of laziness that it repeats, it just repeats.

"The other piece of music I always loved is Bach's Toccata and Fugue in D Minor, which has this hammering between the thumb and the forefingers. So I had the idea of turning that upside down and instead of hammering that way, hammering the other way. The combination of Bach and Terry Riley was a subconscious idea; I just sat down at the organ and instantly played the little opening motif to 'Tubular Bells'.

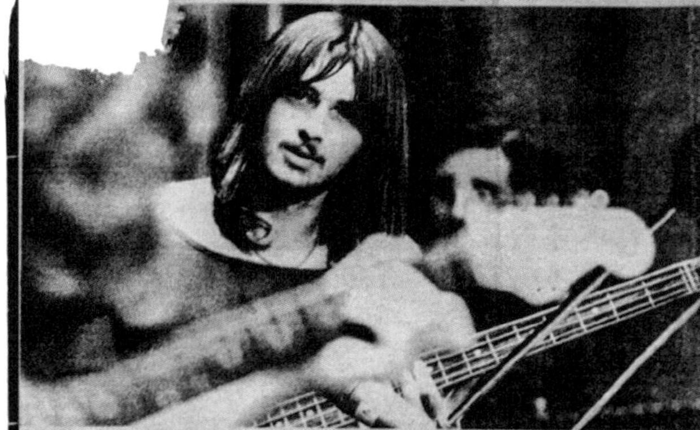

MIKE OLDFIELD'S TUBULAR BELLS

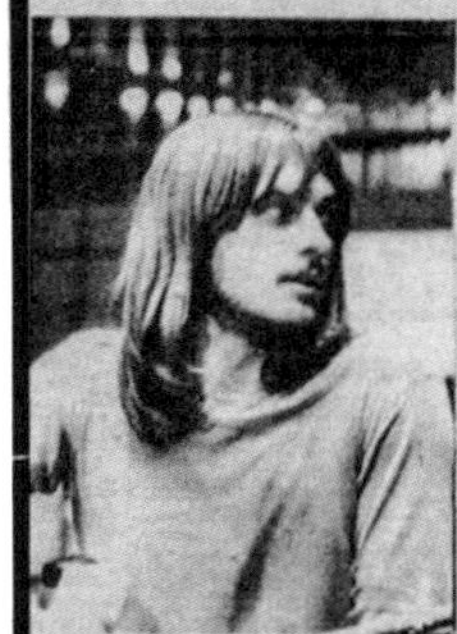

'Tubular Bells' is a vast work, almost classical in its structure and in the way a theme is stated and deftly worked upon. Geoff Brown — Melody Maker.

It is not often that you get in a batch of the first releases from a new record company and find among them an album that not only strikes you with its freshness of ideas and excellence of execution, but surpasses your expectations of the artist concerned. But Mike Oldfield's 'Tubular Bells' (Virgin V2001) does all that and more. Steve Peacock — Sounds.

I can't think of another album that I'd as unhesitatingly recommend. Steve Peacock — Sounds.

I do not think that words could ever do justice to this beautiful, beautiful music, nor praise it unough. William Murray — Time Out.

Without borrowing anything from established classics or descending to the discords, squeals and burps of the determinedly avant-garde, Mike Oldfield has produced music which combines logic with surprise, sunshine with rain. John Peel — The Listener.

It is one of the most mature, vital, rich and humorous pieces of music to have emerged from the pop idiom. One hearing should provide sufficient proof. Al Clark — NME.

His musicianship throughout the album is flawless and Oldfield amazes the listener with the seemingly never-ending list of instruments he plays. Music Week.

It moves me to the same immensity of feeling as Sibelius or Debussy. It is a major work, and an exquisite achievement. William Murray — Time Out.

It represents the first breakthrough into history that any musician regarded as primarily a rock musician has made. John Peel — The Listener.

An enjoyable, evocative album which bodes well for the future of both the country's newest label, and of Mike Oldfield. Geoff Brown — Melody Maker.

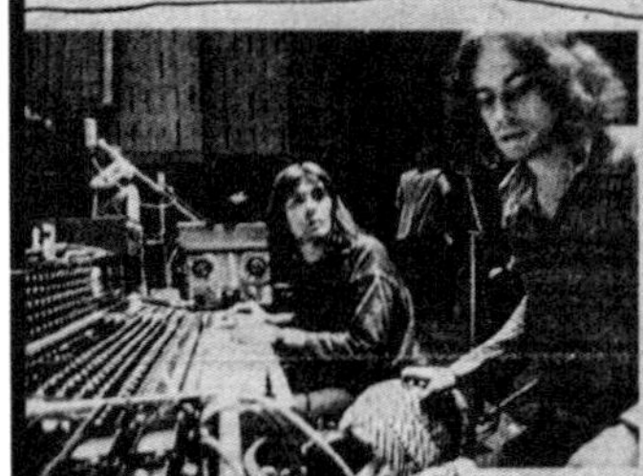

Tom Newman and Simon Heyworth

ROCK MAY now be established as a serious art form but it is remarkable how few lengthy rock works have yet been written. There's The Who's "Tommy," the Electric Prunes' almost forgotten "Mass in F minor," two excellent works by the Pink Floyd, one by Emerson, Lake, and Palmer, and one by Jethro Tull. Suddenly there are two more. Tonight there's the first live performance of Mike Oldfield's fascinating "Tubular Bells," while over the weekend Jethro Tull twice packed the Empire Pool, Wembley, for their new and less impressive rock opus, "A Passion Play."

MIKE OLDFIELD'S "Tubular Bells" is a rock masterpiece, and will be remembered as one of the handful of major works that has broken the musical barriers and created a new art form. I do not claim this as an original judgment—I share it with several critics who have reviewed the album of this work—but it is certainly one that needs a lot of explanation, particularly in this branch of the music business where extravagant praise and blame is bandied around so easily that it almost becomes meaningless. So, why a "rock masterpiece." ?

Because this is one of the first works that not only blends classical and rock styles but uses a large variety of instruments as a highly successful rock orchestra. In the past, this term has meant either complementing a group with some tired clichés from the strings of the LSO, adding a powerhouse of horns to a soul singer, or meandering towards big-band jazz like Frank Zappa.

Oldfield uses rock instruments—particularly a string quartet of electric guitars and bass—to create their own sound, to which he adds organ and woodwind. It is a new concept of "classical music" (for want of a better term) and not a weak electric imitation.

Oldfield's record was remarkable for the fact that he played almost all the instruments himself and put the whole thing together with 2,000 overdubs. It was a technical triumph but became a little too slick in the process. Last night, for his first live performance at the QEH, Oldfield played guitar and bass and was joined by a girl choir and 16 musicians including guitarist Mick Taylor of the Rolling Stones. The effect was devastating.

The Guardian

MIKE OLDFIELD'S "Tubular Bells" was one of those rare and charming experiences believed all but lost to the London music scene. In an age of endless "great little rock and roll bands" desperately projecting egos at all angles, it was a pleasure to hear a whole crew of mixed musicians — rock and classical — sublimating their talent to the art of a composer.

There were no flashy, long-winded solos, no exhibitions of stamina or endurance, at London's Queen Elizabeth Hall on Monday night. Instead, there was a co-operative contribution to the mood-weaving, fragile jollity of Oldfield's two-part invention for rock musicians and string section.

There were some patrons slightly disappointed that the assembly of talent didn't jam in the usual fashion, but this would have destroyed the meaning and purpose of Mike's outstanding composition. Virgin Records and Mike Oldfield should be congratulated for taking a bold plunge into the non-commercial aspect of rock music. — CHRIS WELCH

When on Monday evening, the entire audience at the Queen Elizabeth Hall rose to its feet and hollered for more, it was one of those rare spontaneous outbursts of appreciation. It was the power of performance and the splendour of the music that motivated such response.

Oldfield's music is a total upper — but without resorting to those false histrionics and predictable bum-shakin' devices. The name Mike Oldfield may not mean too much at the present moment, but if he continues to sustain the quality of both his album and this concert, he will eventually emerge as one of the most rewarding leaders of the musical vanguard of the 70's.

Indeed, I can see a time when the name Oldfield will become synonymous with a whole original concept in contemporary music.

ROY CARR

MICK JAGGER was in an affable mood at a reception after Mike Oldfield's "Tubular Bells" concert at Queen Elizabeth Hall on Monday

"There's so much good music being played at the moment. I'd really like to do a concert like this one.

— Melody Maker.

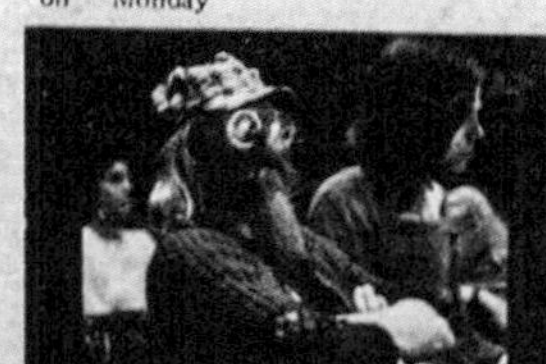

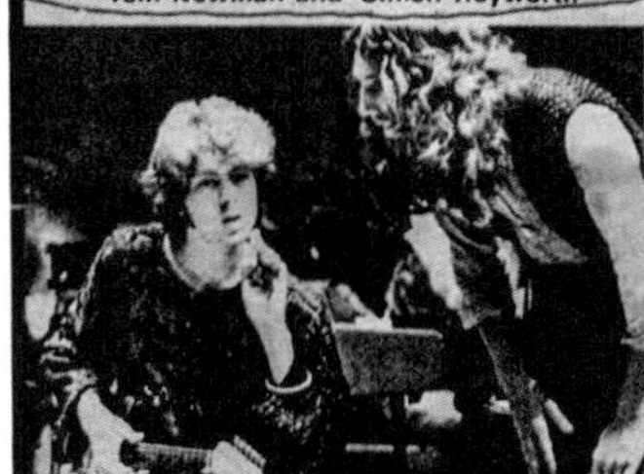

Mick Taylor and Steve Hillage

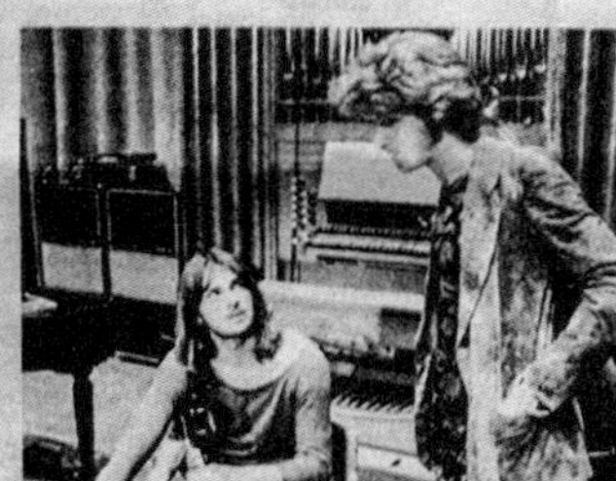

Mike Oldfield Mick Taylor

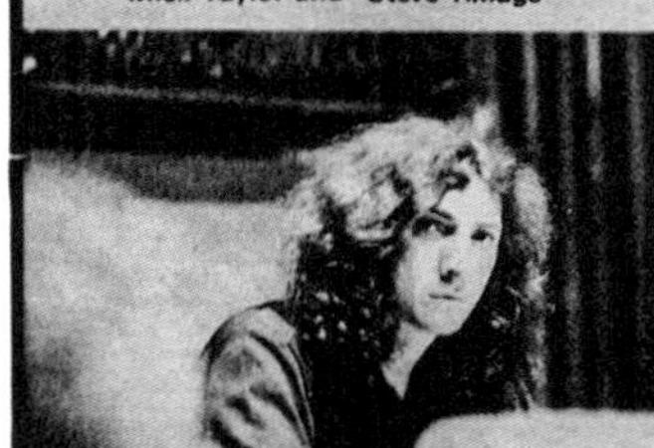

John Greaves

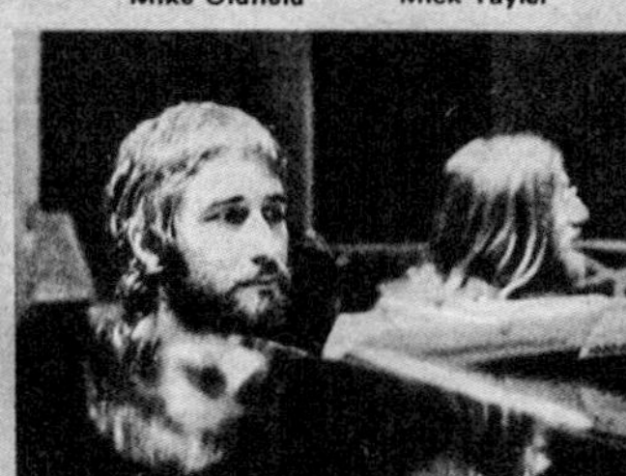

David Bedford

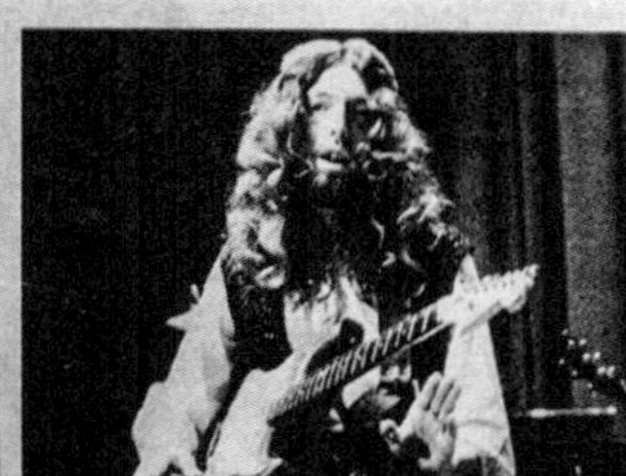

Steve Hillage

Available now from all record retailers

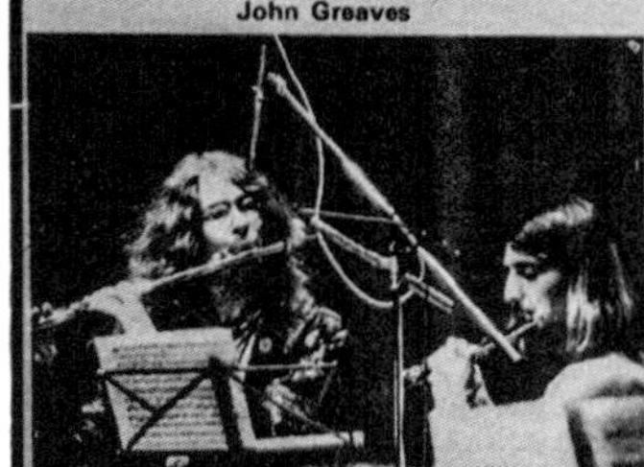

Jeff Leigh and Terry Oldfield

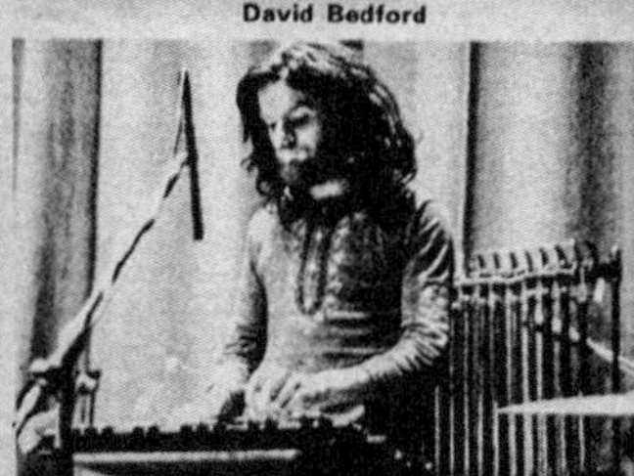

Pierre Moerley

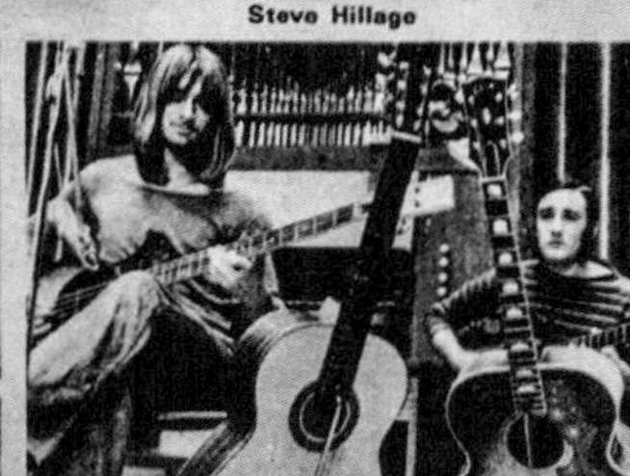

Mike Oldfield and Fred Frith

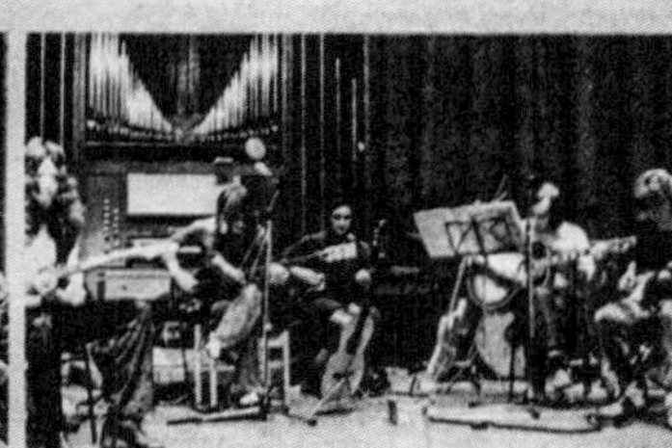

Steve Hillage, Mike Oldfield, Fred Frith, Ted Speight, Mick Taylor

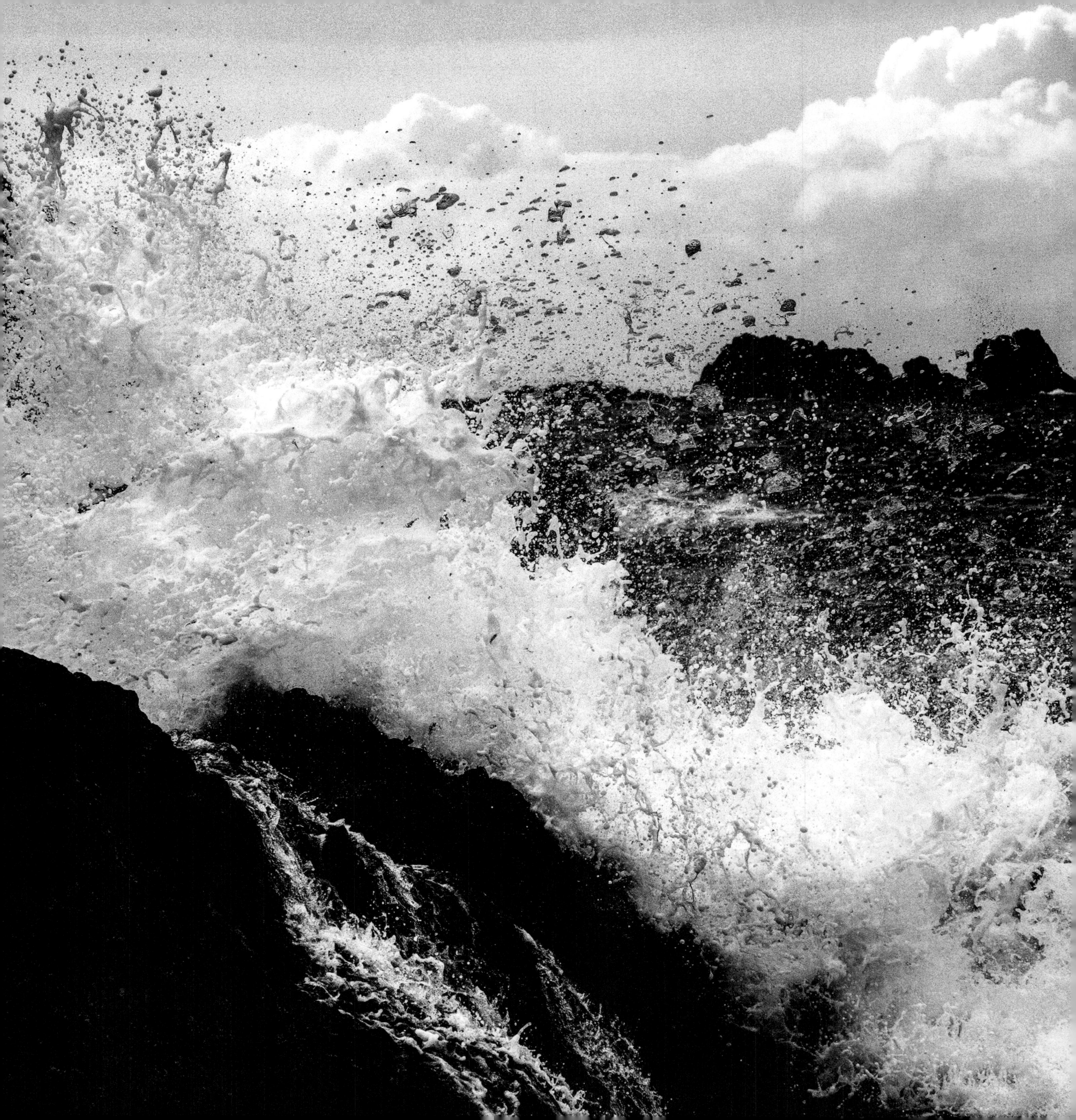

" 'Tubular Bells' was, in fact, quite well rehearsed." MIKE OLDFIELD

"I didn't want it to be straight 4/4 because I find music that you can tap your feet to or dance to really dissatisfying. I like music in odd times, which drops beats and is not perfect. I want to drop beats and cut bits off it and make odd time signatures so that the whole of the first part of 'Tubular Bells' is one bar of seven and one bar of eight. It doesn't feel awkward to me, but if you tried to dance to it you'd fall over.

"I always knew it would be a success. I remember, I had just done that introductory bit and I was going for a walk all round Tottenham in some park or other and picturing in my mind what the reviews of 'Tubular Bells' were going to be – it wasn't even called 'Tubular Bells' at that time. I was imagining that it would be number one in the charts and would be a very popular piece of music. Whether you call it a premonition or what, I believed and saw it all happening. As it turned out it happened exactly as I thought it would.

" 'Tubular Bells' was, in fact, quite well rehearsed. Not only had I had the whole of my life up to the age of 19 to practise it and to write it, but there was also this long period in between the demos and the final recording where I wasn't doing anything. So I liked to spend the whole day practising, playing the piano and the guitar and practising all the parts. When we came to do it, I had a pretty good idea of what I was going to do. There was a little bit of experimentation, but I had the thing mapped out in my head.

"I tried all sorts of different ways of working. I tried being really spontaneous and that works well. I get into this creative frenzy, the eyes go really round and they glaze over and I can get really irritable and grumpy if I play things wrong. I spent most of the time in the studio shouting and screaming at myself. I feel frustrated when I make a mistake or when I can't play it right. But 'Tubular Bells' was very well rehearsed, so there wasn't a lot of that.

"A lot of people used to say, 'I don't know how you managed to get away with no drums, until the bit of Caveman drums on side two'. But when they come in it's really special. I was never conscious of the fact that we ought to put drums on it at all. What I do remember is that after I'd finished it totally, I got a phone call from Richard Branson saying, 'We took it down to Midem (the music business equivalent of the Cannes Film Festival) and somebody said it would be good if it had vocals on it.' Just about that time I went into hospital to have all my teeth out and my face blew up like a balloon. All I could think about was them wanting to put vocals on my piece of music!

"With the Caveman song I just remember having a really good backing track, but didn't know what the hell to put on top of it. I remember we'd come back from the pub and I'd had half a bottle of whisky. I just said, 'Give me the microphone' and we turned the tape speed up, so it was coming through really fast. I was bellowing and making noises. I didn't know what the hell I was doing. It was all done in one take and I screamed myself so hoarse that I couldn't sing for about a week. It was totally spontaneous and wasn't planned at all.

“

The idea for ‘Tubular Bells’ first came when I was working as a bass player in Kevin Ayers’ group Kevin Ayers & The Whole World. We just happened to be at the same venue as this huge jazz orchestra … . That was the first time I had ever seen or heard a long piece of music.

MIKE OLDFIELD

"I think whatever humour is in the record came partly from Kevin Ayers' attitude to himself. His attitude was that he didn't really care, and although he wasn't humorous he did have a very wry sense of humour. He had an attitude that you shouldn't be too stiff and snooty and take yourself really seriously. That's why there are bits of humour in 'Tubular Bells'. Also, with Tom Newman I had a lot of laughs. We just got on together as friends and spent quite a lot of the time laughing and that's very important in a studio. There's no way you can be too serious while you're actually playing; if you make a mistake, you laugh about it.

"There's a moment in the middle of 'Tubular Bells' when a pub piano comes in. I think that was crucial. Of course, Monty Python was around at that time and that kind of humour was an obvious influence.

"It was a very strange time when 'Tubular Bells' became successful. I was uneasy in my mind, in my soul really. I didn't like being in the city. I didn't like a lot of noise and I wanted to live somewhere clean and natural. The possibility existed of me having some money for the first time ever in my life. It wasn't a lot, but I could afford to look for a house.

"I went travelling all the way around Herefordshire because I liked it up there and I ended up in a little house on the edge of a hill at a really wild place. I started writing more music. Meanwhile, 'Tubular Bells' was going to the top of the charts everywhere in the world. The bloody telephone kept ringing – 'You've got to come to America, you've got to go on tour, you've got to do this, we've got to do interviews' etc. I just covered the bloody thing with cushions because all I wanted to do was to look out onto the peaceful Welsh landscape, just for peace of mind."

The success of 'Tubular Bells' made Oldfield uneasy, especially as his name started to become known.

Mike Oldfield: "I didn't have any confidence as a person at all. I felt very insecure and insignificant, scared of the world. If I went into a shop and wanted, for example, to buy a camera, I would say, 'Have you got any cameras?' and the guy would be really fed up with me instantly; but when he recognised my name on the chequebook, his attitude totally changed. I found that really confusing.

"Even the people at The Manor began to change towards me. I really don't understand why. I was the same person, but when you're successful and well known the world changes around you. I found that totally terrifying. I had another breakdown and started drinking too much and hiding away. Richard Branson wanted me to go on tour and that was the last thing I wanted to do.

"He wanted me to travel, to go to America, but I should have been in some sort of care because I was really, really messed up.

"There was a lot of pressure to do a follow-up to 'Tubular Bells'. They even thought of a title for the new album, they wanted to call it something like 'Slipstream'. But I had finished with 'Tubular Bells'. I put such a lot into it that for the moment I wanted to go off in a different direction, a more healthy type of feeling, maybe a bit more classical, very spacious music. 'Tubular Bells' was a lot of confusion, it had a lot of jazzy bits and I wanted to have something which was calmer, bigger and more grand; a bit like the countryside where I was living, which was really beautiful with open hills.

"I got the feeling that when they heard my next record, 'Hergest Ridge', they thought: 'Oh, don't know about this'. As it turned out it got very bad reviews, but it seems to have become quite popular in its time. People still buy it. But they wanted me to do a 'Tubular Bells II' then, which I didn't want to do. But of course that annoyed everybody because they were watching all these potential millions of pounds just disappear. The unco-operative artist just wouldn't co-operate with any of that."

With Oldfield reluctant to promote it by touring, Branson had to get publicity for 'Tubular Bells' another way.

Mike Oldfield: "'Tubular Bells' was already successful when Richard called up saying, 'Somebody wants to use it in a film which is going to be very successful; we can't stop them anyway.' So I thought, 'Oh great!' The next thing I heard it was in 'The Exorcist' and people were coming out of cinemas and going mad. It was a bit scary and I didn't like it.

"Actually I only saw 'The Exorcist' a couple of years ago and I felt it was a very well made film, but I couldn't help imagining the cameraman and how they had made it. I only saw it as a technical thing, I wasn't scared at all. In fact for bits of it I was on the floor laughing because it was so funny. But I would say again that 'Tubular Bells' would have been just as successful without its use in the film."

Mike Oldfield's confidence in the power of the album is as strong now as then.

Mike Oldfield: "I wouldn't change anything about 'Tubular Bells'. And I'm glad that piece of music will live and have a life of its own, independent of my life. People will hopefully be listening to it for many, many years to come. Also I think it's been influential. What disappoints me is that

"I wouldn't change anything about 'Tubular Bells'. And I'm glad that piece of music will live and have a life of its own, independent of my life." MIKE OLDFIELD

it hasn't sparked enough instrumental music; people aren't playing music for its own sake. I'd like to be an ambassador for instrumental music and I would like to see a lot more instrumental music than there is today.

"For instance, I've always been fascinated by bagpipes which is why I did the thing with the Hoover. I don't know why, I just love bagpipes. It's always been my dream to have a guitar sounding like bagpipes, which now of course you can do with today's technology. But I tried all sorts of things to get an electric guitar to sound like bagpipes to the extent that I developed my own way of playing. I always put little grace notes in front of notes, but the only reason bagpipes have these grace notes is because you can't stop Scottish bagpipes making a noise. It's got to be a continuous sound, because there's no way of stopping the chanter chanting. So it sounds awful without grace notes. And by some coincidence I picked that technique up.

"I also get the sound as clean as possible. It's to do with the fact that I always fingerpick when I play; I hardly ever play with a plectrum. That comes from my acoustic guitar playing, which is a bit like classical guitar, because you're doing everything with fingernails. But doing it like that, you can mute any string that's not actually being played.

"Just about every electric guitarist I've seen always puts too much vibrato on a string. A violinist, though, creates vibrato in a different way, so I use a violin-type vibrato. I also use a lot of overdrive and a lot of distortion through the guitar amp, so you get a sound which is something like a bagpipe reed.

"I have no problem playing electric guitar in the studio; I can pick it up and quickly play something acceptable. Other instruments, like piano, which I'm not so good at, take longer, but guitar is not really any problem.

"We had great fun with the first effects box, though. This was a Glorfindel box (Glorfindel is a character from J R R Tolkien's *The Lord of the Rings*) which was brought into the studio. It was a funny little wooden contraption and I couldn't believe it. I thought I might be able to make that sound like bagpipes if I plugged the guitar in to it. It was a startling piece of equipment, like that contraption in 'ET' and somehow the sound that came out was this absolutely squeezed flat, lovely bagpipe sound.

"But some of the keyboards you can get now! I couldn't believe it when I got one of those keyboards and played a couple of notes. All the component sounds of the 'Tubular Bells' introduction were there, just at the touch of a button. You hear variations of 'Tubular Bells' all the time on commercials, film scores or anything that uses music which hammers between notes. If you listen for it you'll hear it all the time, anywhere in the world. It's become soaked into the culture.

"... everything I had lived, all adolescence, childhood, happiness, disappointment, laughter and tears, was all encapsulated in that piece of music." MIKE OLDFIELD

"I'm especially proud of the fact that 'Tubular Bells' is good, especially in the way that the sections join together. There was always something that carried over and joined it so beautifully. I do have a slightly sad feeling that I didn't appreciate its success, because I was so scared of it, I was too young.

"It was probably very lucky for me that I did keep out of the way, because I've got to know this music business in the last 20 years and it's quite a hard business, very vicious. There are some dishonest people in it and it's quite cut-throat, really. I would have been taken for a ride left, right and centre by just about everybody if I'd gone out and worked and toured the world. I was psychologically unfit for it, so I did the best thing I could, which was to sit out in my shack on the edge of the Welsh hillside and write music.

"I think that record was almost like encoding or recording or encapsulating an entire human personality, a human life; all that range of emotions and experiences. Even though I hadn't had much of a life up until then, because I was so young, everything I had lived, all adolescence, childhood, happiness, disappointment, laughter and tears, was all encapsulated in that piece of music.

"We had a lot of love and a 100% conviction and I suppose it was an act of desperation: I had to do it. That gives the piece a life of its own, a soul, some sort of spiritual feeling. That's the only way I can describe it."

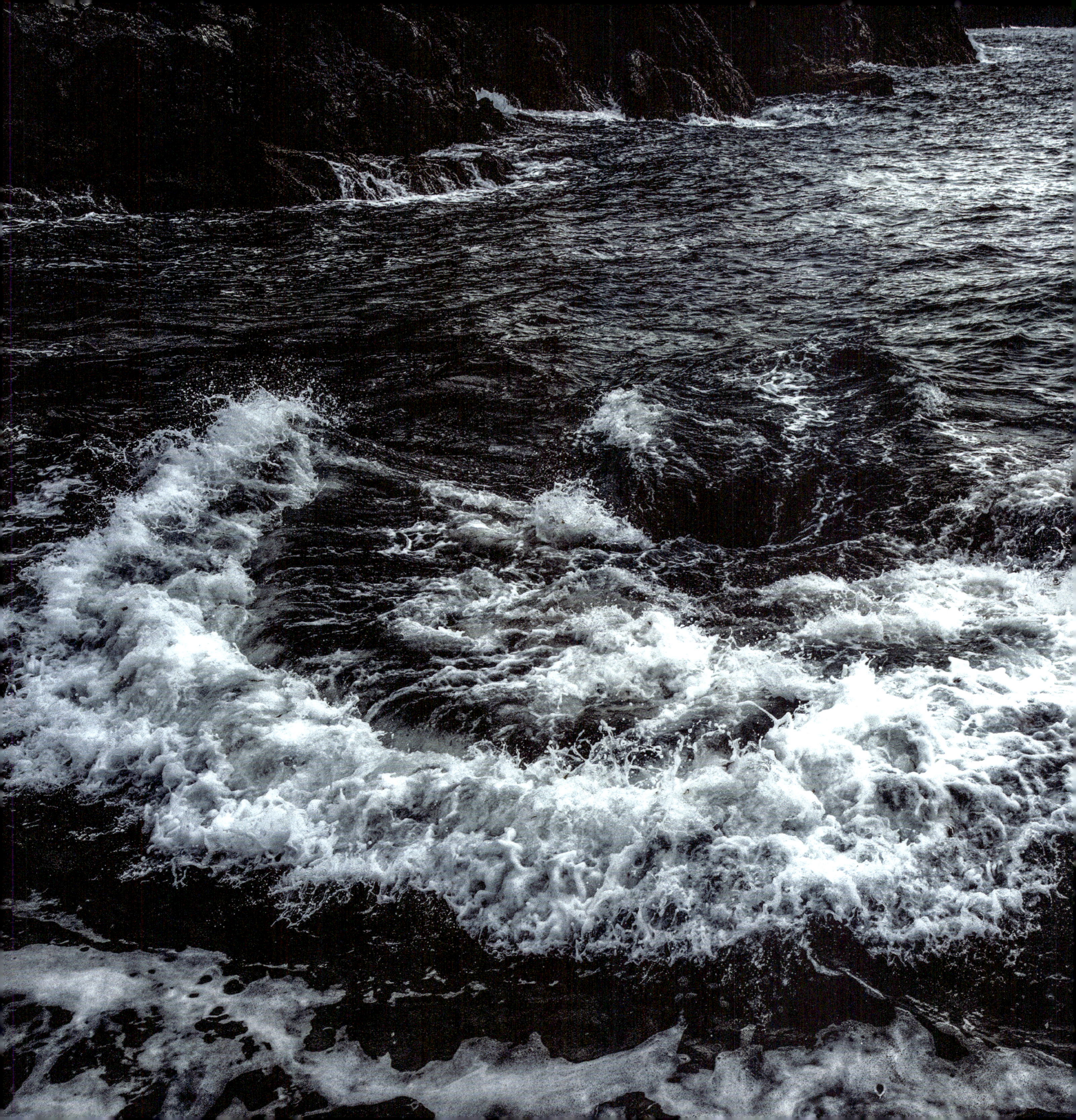

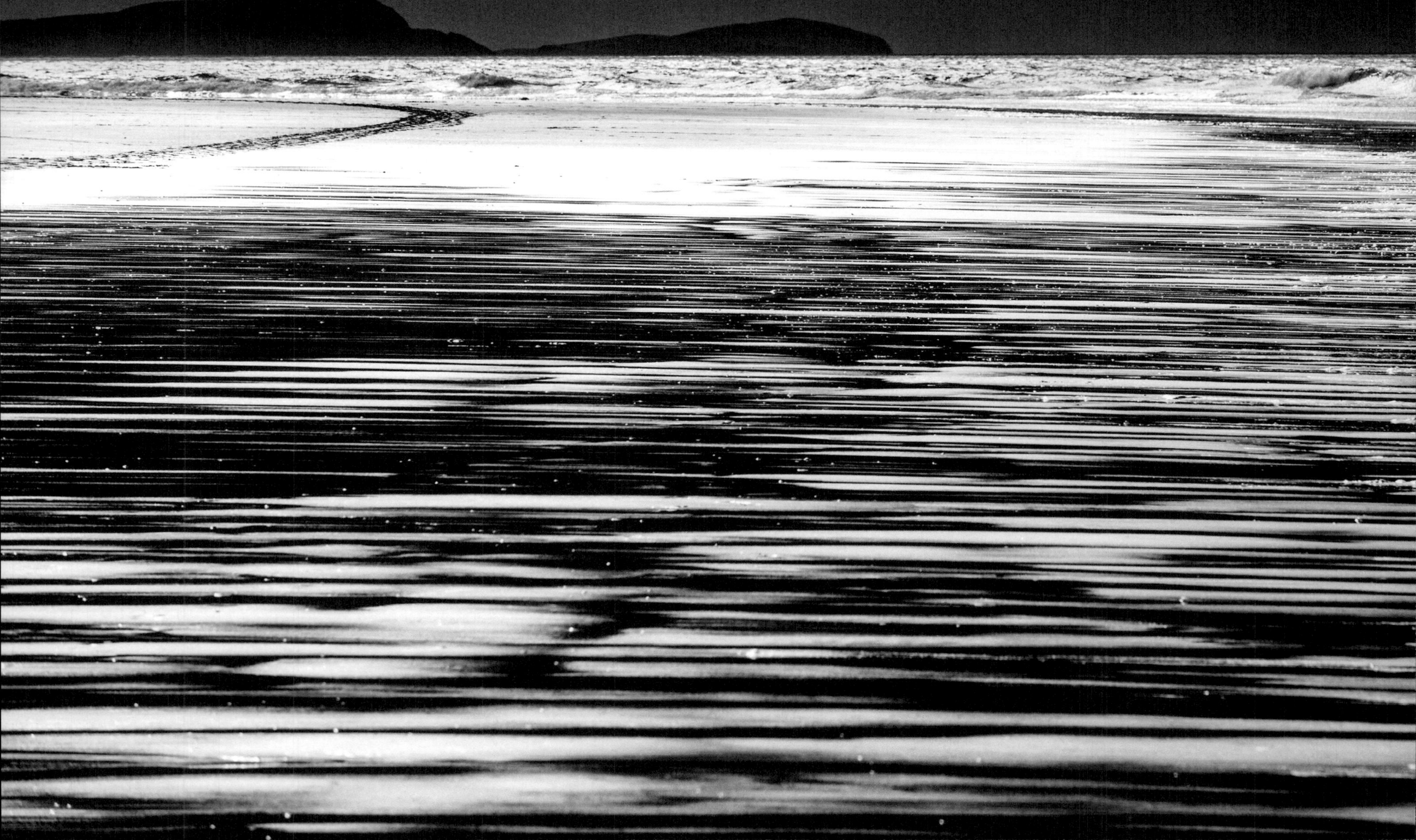

6 EPILOGUE

*H**ISTORY** will confirm that 'Tubular Bells' went on to become an enormous success. In many ways it is a piece of music which stands alone, outside of fashion and passing time. It has survived through many changes in music and the music industry. Richard Branson has acknowledged its importance many times in allowing him the cash flow to expand the Virgin empire.*

Mike Oldfield remained with Virgin Records for almost 20 years, creating many other records. Eventually he left the company which Richard Branson then sold to EMI, in March 1992, for £560,000,000.

After leaving Virgin, Mike Oldfield found a new manager and signed to WEA records. His first release, ironically enough, was a new version of the original work. 1992 saw the debut of 'Tubular Bells II' which has sold in excess of three million copies.

Simon Heyworth has since worked with a wide array of genres and artists, eventually founding his own revolutionary studio Super Audio Mastering in 2002.

Tom Newman went on to be a successful freelance record producer, working with a number of major artists, and is co-credited with Trevor Horn as producer of 'Tubular Bells II'.

Mike Oldfield is now a competent and successful musician in his early 60s, secure in the knowledge that his records are destined to remain 'marketable' for a long time to come.

RICHARD NEWMAN
Cambridgeshire 2017